'In the annals of mission, the nam[e]
not necessarily be visible alongside Carey, ...
but her story needs telling, in praise of the grace of God, ...
tribute to a life selflessly lived for the gospel and because Audrey stands as one of the countless faithful missionaries down through the years who are unknown by most, but famous to God. My prayer is that her example of life-long commitment to the cause will inspire more Careys, Judsons, Taylors and Featherstones.'

John Brand. *Having been in the pastoral ministry for some 12 years, John worked for 14 years with AIM International (founded as Africa Inland Mission), serving as their European director. At the end of August 2007 he joined the Faith Mission and John became vice principal of the Faith Mission Bible College in Edinburgh.*

'When Elleea and Audrey Featherstone began to attend our services at Lansdowne I soon sensed that, though quiet and unassuming, here were two of those top quality dedicated Christian missionary warriors who bore in their bodies and minds a lifetime of joys and sorrows, blessings and sufferings, from a land far away. I only wish now I could have spent more personal time with them. However, I am grateful to Tim Shenton for telling this extraordinary story of an 'ordinary' lady. We constantly need to be reminded of what it means to live a life of total consecration to Jesus Christ. Here we have perseverance, love, toil, joy, fear, danger — and abundant fruit, which will last through eternity. I wish this book wide circulation and pray it will be both a challenge and blessing to many, many readers — as it has been to me.'

Harry Kilbride, *pastor of Lansdowne Baptist Church, Bournemouth, from 1976-1982*

'This is an honest account of an ordinary woman who made an extraordinary impact for the kingdom of God. Against a background of hardship and deprivation, insurrection and life threatening rebellion as Congo moved towards independence, Audrey courageously lived out her Christian faith. The circumstances of her early life, in the UK and then in Congo, are barely comprehensible in our comfortable ease loving generation. Her simple 'risk all' obedience was an expression of grateful obedience to the Lord who loved her and saved her. The church in the UK needs to take on board and live out this radical commitment to Christ, whatever the cost and wherever the commitment, if we are to see the kingdom of Christ advance in power.'

***David Pickard** went to Thailand in 1970 and worked for four years at Manorom Christian Hospital before becoming Thailand field director from 1976-1984. He then served as director for overseas ministries (OMF's work in Asia) and later as the general director of OMF.*

'Reading this humble account of a life dedicated to the Lord has re-energized my own commitment to missions. I had forgotten the daily challenges of living in an alien culture far from home surrounded by diseases and an unstable government.'

Marc Erickson, *senior pastor of Eastbrook Church, Milwaukee, Wisconsin, USA*

Audrey Featherstone, I presume?

AUDREY FEATHERSTONE, *I Presume?*

THE AMAZING STORY OF A CONGO MISSIONARY

TIM SHENTON

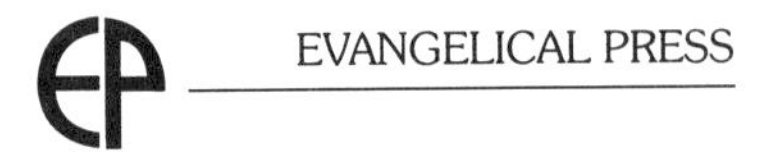

Evangelical Press
Faverdale North Industrial Estate, Darlington, DL3 0PH England
email: sales@evangelicalpress.org

Evangelical Press USA
PO Box 825, Webster, NY 14580 USA
email: usa.sales@evangelicalpress.org

www.evangelicalpress.org

First published 2008

Printed and bound in Great Britain by Biddles Ltd,
King's Lynn, Norfolk

British Library Cataloguing in Publication Data available

ISBN-13 978 0 85234 678 5

Dedicated to that long line of missionaries,
who have trodden a dark and dangerous, yet glorious path
to spread the gospel of Christ in Africa.
We thank God for them.

Contents

'What the state has done for Congo and its people, posterity shall judge. What the missionaries have done, I am seeing with my own eyes, and seeing, I am prouder of my fellow countrymen and women than I have ever been before. Every work of progress and civilization the Congo has seen has owed its inception to, and has been brought to fruition by, these fine people. If from the depths into which the natives have sunk through oppression and neglect, men and women have been brought to a level of good citizens, the missionaries have done it. All that is best in this land is the work of missionaries.'

Edgar Wallace, journalist and writer

Foreword

After reading this remarkable account of an 'ordinary lady', shaped indeed by the hands of an 'extraordinary God', one is reminded of the stories of former missionary heroines, such as Mildred Cable, Francesca French or Gladys Aylward. A rare breed indeed! Such stalwarts possessed an element of fortitude, determination and endurance in the midst of almost insurmountable difficulties, without flinching in the fight. Qualities such as these are now very difficult to find in the lives of modern missionaries, who, it seems, need to be surrounded by all their creature comforts before they even embark on missionary enterprise. But Cable, French and Aylward, spiritual giants in their own right, were prepared to face disease, disaster, danger and disappointment at every turn; they were prepared to take their coffins with them as part of their luggage!

Woven into the fabric of this gripping story of Audrey and her husband Elleea is a series of graphic pictures that clearly portray their lives and witness, together with that of other fellow missionaries engaged in pioneer outreach to people who had never heard of the 'good news' of Jesus Christ.

We read of various encounters Audrey and Elleea experienced, relating to their privations, their sufferings, their quite remarkable response and their reactions in confronting disease, a different climate, language and culture. Such experiences were compounded by communication problems, at times with their own missionary colleagues, and with local believers. Perhaps most painful of all for Audrey and her husband was their forced evacuation from hostile areas where even some believers became turncoats. This was exacerbated by the strain of handing over to what appeared to be an unprepared local church leadership. Many church leaders were strongly influenced by the rising tide of fanatical nationalism, which took no account of the good works and witness of the Christian ambassadors among them. There followed a persecution of local believers, who were now identified by their fellow countrymen as partners with the so-called imperialist colonialist missionary. Faithful local leaders became targets, suppressed and even martyred. The following lines seem to capture the atmosphere where Audrey was working: 'Audrey felt they should return to continue their work with the hundreds of villages deep in the forest, where tribal languages, not French, were spoken. Congo was still in a time of transition, however. The political situation was unstable, the infrastructure was damaged almost beyond repair, and many of the roads were impassable.'

In summary, this well written and well-documented book is a must for aspiring cross-cultural Christian workers. It has deep missiological lessons for those serious in seeking the advance of the gospel in difficult and hostile situations. Those interested in missionary outreach will glean so many lessons, and will thus be able to identify with difficulties missionaries face on the field today. This excellent book should be on the shelf and in the hands of us all. When you put it down, you will no doubt say — 'What an extraordinary God! What an extraordinary person! What an extraordinary book!'

As a result of this book, may the Lord light a flame in the hearts of young and old to fulfil the great commission, so that 'this gospel of the kingdom may be preached as a witness to all nations, and then the end will come' (Matthew 24:14).

Dr John Davis *was a missionary with OMF in Thailand for twenty-five years. He founded Phayao Bible College in North Thailand in 1966 and served there for sixteen years before lecturing at Moorlands College (near Bournemouth, England) as director of cross-cultural studies. He has written books in English on Contextualization and Buddhism, and in Thai, one of which is used by all the Bible Colleges in Thailand.*

1
Let me introduce to you...

I had seen Audrey Featherstone in the congregation at Lansdowne Baptist Church in Bournemouth, England, on many occasions. I suppose the generation gap did not allow me to have much, if any, contact with her. She is a lady well into her eighties and old enough to be my mother, if not my grandmother. I had heard a few members of the church speak about her, and all seemed to hold the deepest respect for her, but I had not talked to her myself.

My first encounter

My first real encounter with Audrey was on one Sunday morning in 2004. She was sitting behind me in her usual pew. After the service I turned around and asked her a question. I had heard she was a wise and discerning lady and I was inquisitive to know her views on a certain matter. She responded with such seriousness that I was immediately gripped, not simply by *what* she said, but *how* she said it. She explained to me the reasons behind her answer, and I noted a depth to her words, a discernment that could only come from long experience with the ways of God and an intimate walk with him.

I left the church that morning thoughtful about my conversation with Audrey, a lady who was obviously grieving over the superficial spirituality of the day. I knew then we were 'kindred spirits', and I knew I had to speak with her again.

****

Some twelve months later Audrey was invited to share her testimony from the pulpit on three Sunday evenings. According to the interviewer, it was a 'big effort' to get her to agree to speak, not from any inhibition to share Jesus Christ, but from a reluctance to push herself into the limelight.

Audrey's testimony

The time came for her to climb the pulpit steps. There was a sense of unwillingness in her approach, a hesitancy to stand before the congregation's gaze; but she took her place in front of the microphone and 250 people. She is small in stature, somewhat stern-faced, almost depressive in looks — until she breaks into a beaming smile — and on this occasion she seemed a little nervous as she stood ready to answer the first question. Maybe there were some in the congregation who wondered what a lady in her eighties was doing in the pulpit. What was she going to say?

'Audrey,' asked Sheila Eaton, who had been her friend for over twenty years, 'did you have a sheltered and comfortable upbringing?'

Audrey laughed and tossed her head backwards, as if to try to mask the pain of those early years. She then spoke clearly and honestly about some of her experiences, all the time recalling the faithfulness of God in times of darkness.

As she was speaking and retelling some of her life, there was what I call a spiritual hush among those listening, a sense of the presence of God that is so often missing from our church services today. It was all too quickly broken as the service leader hurried back to the microphone. I wished she had been allowed to speak for longer, for in many ways God had been using her words to touch lives.

By the end of her third talk, she had told the congregation about her seven-week journey to Congo that was 'full of adventures'. The pastor of Lansdowne Baptist Church, Chris Kelly, then asked how long she had stayed in Congo.

'Twenty-five years,' replied Audrey, with great enthusiasm and a big smile on her face.

'I'm sure there are many more adventures you could tell us about those twenty-five years.'

'Yes,' said Audrey firmly.

'It wouldn't be fair for us to ask you to tell us more on Sunday nights, would it?'

'I'm not going to do it,' responded Audrey with a steely determination, 'you know that very well.'

'Yes, I know that,' said Chris, 'but how about writing a book?' This seemed to throw Audrey, who momentarily appeared to be lost for words.

Regaining her composure, she immediately took the attention off herself and said, 'May I just say, Chris, that there is one verse that is so precious to me and precious to many of you [the congregation] and it's from a Psalm of David, where he says, "As for God, his way is perfect"' (Psalm 18:30).

May I write your biography?

Having been captivated by what she said and keen to learn more, and with the words 'how about writing a book' ringing in my ears, I called Audrey to one side after the service and asked her, 'May I write your biography?'

Predictably she shook her head more in disbelief than anything that I should have such a crazy idea of writing about her life. I tried hard to encourage her, pointing out that just as W. P. Livingstone's book *Mary Slessor of Calabar* had been used by God to change the course of her life, so her biography could be used by God to reach into the lives of others. She listened carefully, often with her head bowed, but I knew I was not moving her in my direction. She promised to pray about it, but the initial signs were not good.

About a month later she came up to me in the foyer of the church and said, 'Tim, I've been thinking and praying about what you asked and my answer is no.'

I expressed my disappointment, but I was not surprised. I thanked her for considering my request and said that I respected her decision. I did not feel at liberty to press my case. I went home, disheartened it must be said, and metaphorically speaking put a line through her name.

For the next couple of months, as I was finishing a double biography of two martyrs of the English Reformation, I thought long and hard about who I was going to write on next. Various names were suggested to me: William Perkins, the 'father of Puritanism'; Joseph Alleine, the author of *Alarm to the Unconverted*; a trilogy on Dod, Hildesham and John Rogers and how the Puritan brotherhood developed; but none of the names mentioned reached out and grabbed my imagination.

The answer we wanted

Then one Sunday evening, 'like an angel from heaven', Linda Fox, who had recently retired after serving Lansdowne Baptist Church for thirty years as personal assistant to the senior minister, approached me. She was a trusted friend of Audrey's and was keen to type up some of Audrey's Bible study notes. Audrey had already told her that she had turned down my request to write her biography. Linda asked, 'Tim, am I right in thinking that you were hoping to write Audrey's life story?' From that starting point our conversation centred on the possibility of resurrecting the idea and I left Linda, along with her husband Malcolm, to approach Audrey for a second time.

After some convincing, Audrey agreed to meet with Linda and me, and after a two-hour conversation, in which we allayed some of her fears about the book, she softened and eventually agreed that we could go ahead. We give God the praise.

****

Why was I so keen to write the book? What is my aim in doing so? These are important questions, which every author must ask before he embarks on any project. My reasons are four-fold.

At the top of my list of reasons is because I want to raise the standard of what I call personal Christianity. Today many Christians from the evangelical wing of the church settle for mediocrity in their spiritual walks, in the sacrifices they make for Christ, in the sermons they hear and the books they read, in their obedience to the word of God, in the doctrines they believe, and so on. It is my hope and prayer that by looking at Audrey's life, we will be stimulated into refusing to accept second best when it comes to walking with God; for there is always more of him for us to know, enjoy and experience; there is always another sacrifice we can make in his service and for his glory.

In the words of the Apostle Paul, we must, as individuals who have been redeemed by the blood of Christ, press on to take hold of that for which Christ Jesus took hold of us. Forgetting what is behind and straining towards what is ahead, we press on towards the goal to win the prize for which God has called us heavenwards in Christ Jesus (Philippians 3:12-14).

Secondly, by looking at God's dealings with Audrey, an ordinary lady, we may see how he can take a 'nobody' and use her for his glory and the extension of his kingdom. Gordon M. Guinness in his foreword to Elizabeth Pritchard's work *For Such a Time*, speaking of Regions Beyond Missionary Union (RBMU), Audrey's mission, says, 'Although there are great figures in the story, like Henry Grattan Guinness and F. B. Meyer, for the most part it is the account of what God has done with "ordinary" people, who dared to take Christ at his word and to follow him faithfully, whatever the consequences, in the power of his Spirit.'

Audrey is the first to admit that she is one of those 'ordinary people', which is why she was initially so reluctant to share her story. 'Who could possibly derive any benefit from my life?' she said to me. But with God all things are possible. He is able to take a shepherd boy like David and make him king; he can take a fisherman like Peter and make him an apostle. He is able to use the least of us, the weakest, smallest and the most insignificant for his pleasure. So if you read Audrey's life and come to the knowledge that God is able to use you, whoever you are, the effort it has taken to produce this work will have been worthwhile.

Thirdly, one of Audrey's burdens is that the church is no longer taking the gospel to 'unreached' people groups, which requires life-long commitment. The emphasis today is on short term service, which has its place and its benefits, but I ask:

where is the laying down of one's life in helping the poor in South America for a few weeks and then returning to the luxury of the West? We need stories today of modern missionaries who are prepared to turn their backs on home, family, security, wealth and all that they count dear, in order to win lost souls for Christ — men and women who are ready to travel to the darkest parts of the earth to live with a people they love, and if necessary, to die among them. Audrey is a modern missionary whose heart is Congolese.

Finally, her life story makes a jolly good read. Her dramatic conversion, her experiences during World War II at the time of the London bombings, her adventures on the way to Congo and her twenty-five years of service in that nation make captivating reading. We all love an adventure story and that is what we have in Audrey's life — danger, excitement, romance, fear, heartbreak and so much more.

****

I cannot go any further without sincerely thanking two people in particular. The first, of course, is Audrey Featherstone. Despite her reluctance, she has been open and frank, making it a pleasure to listen to her story and to write it down for the benefit of others. She is truly a 'gem' in God's kingdom, although she will rebuke me for making such a remark. The second is Linda Fox, whose tireless note taking and typing have made my job easy and enjoyable. She is 'top drawer' when it comes to professionalism and efficiency. In every respect she has been a joy to work with and without her assistance and input this biography would not have been written. Her comments about Audrey will demonstrate the respect she holds for the subject of this biography: 'Every so often the Lord brings someone across our path who makes a profound impact on our lives; I'm so grateful that for me Audrey is such a person.'

I must also thank the many people who wrote to me with their anecdotes and thoughts on Audrey. There are too many to mention here, but some of their names appear in the work.

I thank them for their honesty and willingness to share part of their lives with me.

I am indebted to three authors for background information. The first is Joseph F. Conley, whose work *Drumbeats That Changed the World* is a comprehensive history of Regions Beyond Missionary Union (RBMU) and the West Indies Mission. The second is Michele Guinness and her book *The Guinness Legend*. She provides valuable insights into the formation of RBMU and a stirring biography of its founder, Henry Grattan Guinness. The third author is Elizabeth Pritchard. Her book *For Such a Time* traces the first hundred years of RBMU and is a thrilling read. I echo the words of Gordon M. Guinness, found in the foreword of Pritchard's work: 'Most of us, as we read, will feel almost overwhelmed at the spiritual stature and sacrificial abandonment of those early pioneers; and not of them alone, but of the whole long line of faithful men and women who gave their all through the years.' I have quoted from all three works in the following pages.

It only remains for me to ask God's blessing on this book, that in all I have written God's name may be lifted up for men to see and adore. May we decrease as the Saviour of the world, the thongs of whose sandals we are not worthy to untie, is exalted to the highest heavens.

Tim Shenton

2
Converted

A troubled upbringing

Audrey's parents, Mr and Mrs Leslie Wells, both from fine middle-class families, were teenagers when they married, and within nine years five children were born to them. Pat, the oldest, was born in 1921, Audrey was born in Westcliff-on-Sea in 1922, Peter in 1924, Anthony in 1927 and Valerie, the youngest, in 1930. For the first four years of Audrey's life, the large family lived in two different areas of London before moving to Letchworth in Hertfordshire.

Mrs Eleanor Wells struggled to care for five lively children; she was not helped by her mother-in-law, a competent lady, who, in Audrey's eyes, continually criticized her mother for not managing the household finances carefully enough. Even as a toddler Audrey seemed to sense the animosity that both grandparents on her father's side had for her mother. Perhaps, in a child's way of compensating for such feelings, it was why she clung more to her mother than to her father in these early years. When both Audrey's brothers died, Mr and Mrs Wells were understandably devastated. Approximately eighteen months after their terrible bereavement, the family moved to Wellington Road in Leigh-on-Sea in southeast Essex.

Audrey's father worked long hours in the shipping industry in London, which meant he did not get home until around eight o'clock each weekday night. As Mrs Wells often went out in the evenings to see friends, the two hardly saw each other; thus they drifted apart and their love grew cold. At one point Audrey recalled her mother telling her, 'When I'm not here any more, you will miss me!' She had no idea what the words meant, but they made her feel unhappy.

For most of its history Leigh had been a fishing village, although its sheltered position at the mouth of the River Thames encouraged its growth as a port, with international trade and a shipbuilding business. The famous ship, *The Mayflower*, which transported 102 Separatist Puritans from Plymouth to Massachusetts (U.S.A.) in 1620 may have been built in Leigh-on-Sea; it was certainly fitted out there before its journey to Devon.

But as Audrey adjusted to her new home, the adventures of the 'Pilgrim fathers' were far from her mind, especially as there was little communication and harmony between her parents. Then in 1934, when she was only twelve years old, her father called her to one side and explained that mother had left home and was never coming back; she had met another man. Before she left Mrs Wells had arranged for someone to cook the meals and care for the children until their father returned from work each night, but for Audrey nothing could replace the tenderness of her mother's love.

A heart-breaking decision

Pat and Audrey attended Westcliff High School for Girls in Kenilworth Gardens, Westcliff-on-Sea — a school known for its academic excellence as well as its high moral standards. The sisters had lunch at school, while Valerie went and lived for a while with an aunt before moving to a boarding school in Leigh. On weekends Val went out with her father. When they returned, Audrey looked after her until the beginning of the next term. After a year or so they all went to live together in a guesthouse. They had their own rooms and their father ate his evening meal there.

One Christmas, after divorce proceedings had commenced between Mr and Mrs Wells, Pat and Audrey were called into a room, one at a time, and asked the heart-breaking question, 'Whom do you want to live with?' Audrey, who had been missing her mother, said, 'I want to live with my mother.' Nothing

The Mayflower

came of her expressed preference as she actually stayed with her father.

About 1937 the family moved from the guesthouse to their own small chalet bungalow in Blenheim Crescent, Leigh-on-Sea. It was during this period that Audrey's father began to 'come out of his shell'. He made new friends and enjoyed a more social lifestyle. On weekends he occasionally went dancing or roller-skating, and, although he was in his late thirties, he started to go out with an eighteen-year-old local girl, Joyce Vale. She often visited the bungalow and Audrey even met her parents. Some time after Audrey had left home, she discovered that her father and Joyce had married soon after the outbreak of war in 1939 or 1940.

Happier days on the beach

The problems in her family made Audrey confused about life. She felt insecure, with no sense of belonging to anyone, which was heightened when her sister Pat started to commute to London and then got engaged to Ray, whom she later married. To cope with her isolation she went on Sunday mornings with her father for walks along the seafront, ending with the one and a quarter mile stretch along Southend Pier. These were happy times for both Audrey and Mr Wells.

Audrey enjoyed roller-skating and during the long summer months of the 1930s there was nothing she liked more than spending time on the beach at Leigh-on-Sea. On weekends and even late into weekday evenings, she revelled in the delights of the sea. In those days there were no beach huts looking out to the horizon; rather, families and individuals arrived on the beach early and pitched their tents side by side. In this way the 'regulars' built up a kind of community spirit.

At this stage in her young life Audrey had no thought of God. If she had any kind of nominal faith in a Creator, it was in a distant, irrelevant Being, who was unconcerned about a beach-loving girl. She attended morning assemblies at school, where Anglican prayers and part of the Bible were read, and twice a week she had Scripture lessons, but she paid little attention to what was said and none of the Bible stories made any impression on her.

When she was in her early teens, an elderly clergyman and his wife, Rev and Mrs Smith, Independent Anglicans, started to have meetings on the beach at Leigh, teaching the children Christian choruses and other songs. They were a godly, dedicated couple. No matter how hot the weather, Rev Smith wore a long coat and his wife always dressed in black, making them stand out as 'different' from the partially clad sunbathers; but regardless of the peculiarities of their appearance, they had a real heart to win children for Christ. Audrey, who never minded having her 'beach time' disturbed, joined in with the singing, but did not have any individual conversations with them, never went to their church, and from all outward appearances was brought no nearer to a saving faith.

Among those who pitched their beach tent near to Audrey and her family were Mr and Mrs Jimmy Green, a couple in their fifties, whom Audrey got to know quite well. She often went to their home for coffee or a meal and soon a strong bond of friendship grew up between them. They were not Christians, but God was going to use them to pass on some very valuable advice to their new friend. They came from London and Mr Green was still working in the city, commuting each day from Leigh-on-Sea.

Bourne & Hollingsworth

One day Audrey's father announced, 'I'm afraid you must leave school at the end of term.' Audrey was saddened by the news that her education was about to come to a premature end and she cried all the way home after her last day at 'the school she loved'.

In early summer of 1939, when Audrey was sixteen, she managed to get a job as a cashier. After about eight months, with war imminent, her father suggested that she look for 'more suitable work', but she had no idea how to find another job or for what sort of job she was qualified.

In her anxiety she went to the Greens for advice. They gave her the address of a prestigious London department store, Bourne & Hollingsworth, on Oxford Street, and told her to write a letter to the personnel manager. After a few weeks she received an interview date, and on the day in question Mr Green kindly accompanied her to London, promising to pick her up after the interview. Much to Audrey's surprise, she was offered the job. (When Audrey became a Christian in 1940, she wrote and told the Greens about her conversion, but she did not receive a reply. A few weeks later, as she was walking down Bishopsgate, she bumped into Jimmy. Sadly his attitude towards her had changed. He said, 'We don't want to talk to you now that you have become all religious.' They never spoke to her again.)

She was only seventeen when she joined Bourne & Hollingsworth as a junior staff member. She was placed under the charge of the department head, Mr Peters, who gave her a variety of jobs such as serving behind the counter and running errands, which helped her to learn how the large store operated. After she had been there several weeks, she asked if she could learn window dressing, but after two or three months of instruction, it was obvious she did not possess sufficient artistic flair! She was transferred to the accounts department.

Her hours were from 9:00 a.m. to 6:00 p.m. Every day she commuted from Leigh, first by train and then by bus, which took about two hours each way. During the late summer months the long journeys were bearable, but after war broke out in September and the London blackouts started, the trips home were perilous. Under blackout rules, windows were carefully covered at night, street lamps and car headlights were turned off and flashlights were to be used wisely, all in an attempt to make it difficult for German bombers to find their target in the dark. The lack of light meant that pedestrians often bumped into one another, traffic accidents increased and some people drowned as they fell off bridges or walked into ponds. Bus services were restricted or withdrawn altogether to save fuel and to limit working during blackout, and timetables were unpredictable. Under these conditions, it was hardly surprising that Audrey, a timid seventeen-year-old, found the journey home frightening.

Bourne & Hollingsworth

Bourne & Hollingsworth owned an 'excellent and beautiful' hostel in Gower Street called Bourne House, for older staff members who did not live in Central London. Audrey, because of the difficulties she was experiencing getting home, asked if she could 'live in'. Under normal circumstances employees under the age of eighteen were not permitted to stay there, but because of the war and the blackouts, Audrey was given special permission to share a 'lovely' room with another girl. Excellent meals were provided and there was a large communal lounge, which had probably been a ballroom in earlier days.

Miss Cornwall

The hostel was very comfortable and much more convenient, but Audrey was lonely — desperately lonely. She missed her family and had no idea what her father was doing or where her mother was living. Only some years later did she discover that her father and Joyce had moved to Streatham. Unfortunately their marriage did not last.

In the big impersonal city of London she had no friends with whom to spend her free time. Every morning, as she made her way to work, there was a deep ache in her heart. She did not know what it was or why it was there, she just felt *so* empty and it hurt. When weekends came, most of the staff living in the hostel went home, leaving the place eerily quiet. Audrey was lost and alone. On Saturdays and Sundays she went for long walks in the hope that the time would pass more quickly and that her sense of isolation could be kept in check. And so the weeks dragged on.

There was one person, a senior staff member, perhaps recognizing Audrey's sadness, who showed an interest in her and always took the trouble to ask how she was. Her name was 'Miss Cornwall'. That was not her real name, but she came from Cornwall and so was known by that name. There was a snack bar in the hostel and from time to time she invited Audrey to join her for a cup of tea and a chat. Miss Cornwall was a Christian, although she never shared her faith with Audrey at this time.

Converted

In January 1940, bacon, butter and sugar were rationed and Audrey was issued her buff-coloured ration book, which contained tokens that could be saved or used at her discretion. The shopkeeper would remove the tokens before issuing the goods. In March meat rationing came into force.

In the middle of the ever-worsening war crisis (March 1940), Miss Cornwall invited Audrey to the *Prince's Theatre* in Shaftesbury Ave, which had been opened on 26 December 1911. (In 1962 EMI bought the theatre and after a refit and redecoration opened it the following year under a new name: the *Shaftesbury Theatre*.) Audrey was delighted to be going to the theatre, although she had no idea that she was actually being invited to a Christian meeting. Such was the depth of her loneliness, that she was happy to accept an invitation anywhere! So off she went with her friend, through the blacked-out streets of London, to the *Prince's Theatre*.

As Audrey entered the building she was astonished to find it packed, with over a thousand people. The man on the stage at the front speaking to the people may have been Alan Redpath, who joined the National Young Life Campaign as an evangelist in 1936, a position he filled until May 1940 when he was called to be pastor of Duke Street Baptist Church, Richmond, London. But it was the singing that caught Audrey's attention, both the words and the tunes. In fact, the whole atmosphere of that meeting so overwhelmed the teenager from Essex that she could have stayed there forever! Sadly for Audrey, the meeting came to an end. On the way home Miss Cornwall carefully asked, 'Did you enjoy it?' Hardly able to contain herself, she exclaimed, 'Oh yes!' Her friend wisely said nothing else, and Audrey was left elated yet confused, because she did not understand *why* she had enjoyed it so much.

The next evening she hurried back to the *Prince's Theatre*, this time on her own. During the singing she experienced exactly the same feelings of exhilaration and joy that she had experienced the night before. One chorus in particular made a deep impression on her:

Bring him your sorrows
Bring him your tears
Bring him your heartaches
Bring him your fears
Go tell him plainly, just how you feel
Jesus will pardon
Jesus will heal

She left the theatre that Thursday evening with an ever-increasing sense that God was calling her and touching her life, although she had little idea of the significance of what was happening. She could hardly wait for the Friday meeting to begin, which was the last day of the weeklong mission. She sat in one of the seats and listened as she had never listened before, as every word penetrated her heart. As the gospel of Christ was proclaimed, she realized she was 'full of sin and needed a Saviour', but she was still mixed up. On the one hand she felt so empty inside, like a lost little girl — broken and forlorn — and yet on the other, she knew she was hearing words of truth and hope.

At the conclusion of the meeting, without revealing to anyone what was going on in her soul, she rushed back to her room in Bourne House. She sat on the bed and in desperation cried out to Jesus, 'I want you. I want you to be my Saviour. I want to follow you all my life!' It was a prayer that changed her life.

A new life

When she awoke the next morning, she knew that Jesus Christ had heard her prayer. There was lightness in her spirit and the inner ache that had caused her so much sadness had gone. She could think of nothing else but beautiful thoughts of her new Saviour. At this point she did not have a great conviction of sin — she could not even remember if she had asked for forgiveness the night before, but she knew she was now a child of God and that Jesus was real and alive.

What she did remember were the books that had caught her attention in the foyer of the *Prince's Theatre*. She also remembered that during her lonely walks in the St Paul's area of London she had passed many Christian bookshops, which had books similar to the ones at the theatre. So on Saturday afternoon, with an urgency to find out more, she started her search. She went to Ludgate Hill and stepped inside one of the shops, perhaps Marshall, Morgan & Scott. With enthusiasm and a quiet determination to find what she was looking for, she pulled book after book from the shelves.

Suddenly her heart sank as she thought, 'I hardly have any money!' She quickly looked at the prices and found a small, cheap book that she could just afford. It was a hardback of 127 pages called *Life With a Capital 'L'* by Alexander Lindsay Glegg, first published by Marshall, Morgan & Scott in 1934. In it the author reproduces sermons and addresses given by him as a layman at conventions and missions, and shows how the Christian life is a great adventure. He explains what it means to trust in Jesus, and that to become a Christian is to start a new *Life With a Capital 'L'*. All the basics of the Christian faith are covered. Over the next few weeks Audrey bought several other small books, which helped her to grow spiritually, and following their advice, she eventually purchased a Bible.

Dunkirk

These momentous events that were taking place in Audrey's life were running parallel with a momentous event that was taking place in the country; for in late May and early June 1940 some 338,000 allied troops were evacuated from Dunkirk and the surrounding beaches by a variety of motor boats, fishing smacks, trawlers, lifeboats, paddle steamers and many other types of craft that had sailed across the channel to assist the escape. At the time the British Prime Minister, Winston Churchill, described the rescue as 'a miracle of deliverance'. The evacuation ended the first phase in the Battle of France; but while it provided a great boost to British morale, it left the French to stand alone against a renewed German assault southwards. The Nazis entered Paris on 14 June, and France surrendered eight days later. Audrey heard about the evacuation and France's capitulation on a public wireless.

On a personal level Audrey's life was fresh, new and exciting; for she found nothing better than following Jesus and rejoicing in his love and forgiveness. And yet she was only too aware that on a national level, the threat of a German invasion was becoming ever more alarming, and it made her apprehensive about the future. On the wireless it was reported that the British government was conducting a massive programme of military and civilian mobilization, and rapidly constructing field fortifications, which transformed much of the British landscape, especially southern England, into a prepared battlefield. Woefully short of heavy weapons and equipment, the British had to make the best use of whatever resources were available.

Going to church

The contrast in Audrey's mind was stark: the death and decay of the bloody battlefields, and the blossoming spring and summer days, when nature is at its most beautiful. During these months she often returned to her room to write poems about her new life in Christ, but at this stage she never thought of going to church. Then her friend Miss Cornwall told her that she was going home for a holiday and invited Audrey to 'see her off'. Surprisingly, Audrey did not tell her about her faith in Christ or thank her for the part she played in her salvation, a missed opportunity she always regretted. On Saturday, as she accompanied her friend to Paddington Station, Miss Cornwall asked her what she was doing the next day. 'Don't you think it would be good, my dear, if you went to church? I think you should, either St Paul's, Portman Square, or All Souls, Langham Place.'

Audrey waved goodbye, with her friend's final advice running through her mind. As she thought about what Miss Cornwall had said she began to feel guilty for not going to church. She arrived home, but reasoned with herself that she could not possibly go to church because she did not have a hat, and everyone who went to church wore a hat. Besides, she was short of money and it was Saturday evening and all the hat shops were closed.

All Souls, Langham Place

So what should she do? She thought about the time one Sunday morning when she was a girl going to the beach, looking tanned and wearing a swimsuit. She saw a group of people on the other side of the road walking in the opposite direction to church. All the men were dressed in dark black suits and hats, and all the ladies wore long skirts and hats. She thought, 'How peculiar they look!' Some time later she went and found the church building, which was aptly named 'The Peculiar People Chapel, Leigh-on-Sea'! What was firmly in her mind was that people who went to church wore hats, and she was not about to break with tradition. So she waited several weeks until she could afford to buy a hat.

The day came, in the summer of 1940, when Audrey went to church for the first time, and she chose All Souls, an imposing looking structure that had been built by John Nash and opened in 1824. (Soon after Audrey's first visit a land mine caused extensive damage to the church, which had to close for some ten years while repair works were carried out. During this time, the congregation met for worship at St Peter's Church, Vere Street.)

As everyone was going up the steps, Audrey, with her new hat carefully pinned in place, was ushered in. One of the sidesmen asked, 'Are you alone?' and then led her right down to the front in full view of the congregation, making her feel decidedly uncomfortable and conspicuous. The service began and Audrey was completely lost. She did not understand the readings from the Prayer Book or the Bible and, positioned right at the front, she had no idea when to stand or when to sit or when to kneel. She felt so self-conscious that she hoped the ground would open up and swallow her. The evangelical preacher, Rev Harold Earnshaw Smith, made no impression on her. She left the service, not only without receiving any spiritual benefit from her experience, but vowing never to go again.

It was not long, however, before her conscience urged her to go to church again. She could not face returning to All Souls, so she attended Miss Cornwall's other suggestion, St Paul's in Portman Square, where Rev Colin C. Kerr, who founded Campaigners Ministries, an evangelical youth organization, was preaching. She made sure she sat at the back so she could watch and follow everyone else. Thus she started to attend church on a regular basis, morning and evening, but always on her own. She received good teaching and grew in her faith, but it was not long before she started to feel out of place.

3
The bombing of London

The Battle of Britain

In July 1940 the Battle of Britain raged in the skies over southern England and the English Channel as the German Luftwaffe attempted to gain air superiority over the Royal Air Force in preparation for a planned sea and airborne invasion. At first the RAF's 700 or so Spitfire and Hurricane fighters were outnumbered, but with the advantage of the most advanced radar system in the world, and the ability to build planes at an astonishing rate, British pilots, flying more agile aircraft, eventually gained the upper hand.

The following month the Luftwaffe launched attacks of more than 1,000 aircraft at a time, focusing on Britain's airfield and radar installations, but their losses were heavy. By the end of August the Germans had lost more than 600 aircraft and the RAF about 300. Many experienced RAF pilots were killed and the bombing damage done to the radar stations left Britain so vulnerable that if attacks on air installations had continued, the eventual outcome of the battle may have been different; but Hitler shifted the focus of his assaults.

At the beginning of September, Britain retaliated by launching air raids on some of Germany's industrial areas and on Berlin itself. Hitler was furious at such strikes and on 7 September he ordered the Luftwaffe to bomb British cities, especially London and its docks. On that first day of bombing 430 people were killed and 1,600 badly injured. It was the beginning of the Blitz and it continued until May 1941 with devastating effects — 60,000 people lost their lives, 87,000 were seriously injured and two million homes were destroyed. On 15 September 1940 more than 1,000 enemy aircraft carried out a day and night bombing of London, which became known as Battle of Britain Day. The RAF shot down about fifty-six enemy aircraft.

Baptized

During the chaos and carnage of the Battle of Britain and the Blitz, Audrey was still working at Bourne & Hollingsworth, and because she was a timid, quiet person, the spiritual change that had taken place in her life was not immediately apparent to her colleagues. At St Paul's, where she was worshipping, she started to feel uncomfortable and to regard herself as an 'outsider', for there were some parts of the service she still did not understand — when the congregation celebrated Communion, she did not know what they were doing, and as she had never been christened, she imagined she was not 'right' in their eyes; and in many other ways she thought she did not fit in.

She read about baptism in the Bible, but was not sure what it meant. She knew that Jesus had commanded his disciples to be baptized and she wanted to be obedient, but she did not know how to go about it. Her faith was so personal that she did not dare speak to anyone about it. She cried out to the Lord, 'How can I be baptized?'

It was about November 1940, when Miss Muriel Hawkes at Bourne & Hollingsworth approached her one Saturday. 'Audrey,' she inquired, 'would you like to come with me to church tomorrow? We have been having some special speakers and I wonder whether you would like to come with me to the concluding meeting.'

Audrey had spoken to Miss Hawkes only once or twice previously, but she immediately replied, 'Yes!' with great enthusiasm, so thrilled was she to be going to church *with* someone.

The next evening they met in the hall and then walked westwards across Euston Road and disappeared into the back streets. Everywhere was so dark because of the blackouts. They arrived at the church, a small Brethren Hall, and went inside. There were about 100 in the congregation, including many young people, and all were singing with great gusto. Then, amazingly, the preacher stood up and said, 'I am going to speak about baptism. The next step for anyone who has come to faith in Christ is baptism.' Well, Audrey nearly fell off her seat when she heard the topic of the sermon.

At the end of the meeting Miss Hawkes introduced Audrey to the preacher, who asked, 'How can I help you?'

'I want to be baptized!' said Audrey.

'Well, tell me your story.'

So, for the first time Audrey poured out the story of her salvation and why she wanted to be baptized. After listening carefully for some time, he said, 'I will baptize you next Sunday night.'

Next Sunday duly arrived, and to her obvious delight Audrey was baptized along with three or four others. Her baptism text was: 'Thy shoes shall be iron and brass; and as thy days, so shall thy strength be' (Deuteronomy 33:25).

Audrey only attended the Brethren Hall twice. She returned to St Paul's, but did not really talk to anyone about spiritual matters. She read many books in her spare time, but the printed page did not fill her need for companionship. To a certain extent she still felt lonely, though not unhappy. She had no confidence in herself and missed the security of family life. When her work colleagues spoke about their families, she felt awkward and was unresponsive.

Air raids

There were a couple of girls living at Bourne House, who sometimes went in the evening to amateur dramatics to perform Shakespearian and other plays. Audrey joined them for a short while before the bombing of London closed down that activity.

At Bourne House, when the electrically powered air raid sirens sounded their distinctive warning — a rising and falling signal, created by varying the power to the siren — sometimes in the middle of the night, Audrey and the other lodgers rushed down to the basement, where it was safe. There they sat and waited, quietly listening to the 'thud thud' of heavy bombs pounding nearby buildings. They did not emerge until the second siren sounded the 'all clear', a single, continuous note. After a night of bombing, Audrey stepped into the street and stood aghast at the destruction before her eyes. 'What is happening?' she whispered to herself in a dazed shock. Perhaps surprisingly, she did not feel frightened during the Blitz.

One sight she remembered vividly was the huge silver barrage balloons, set at heights of up to 1,500 metres, filling the London skies. Each balloon was moored to a wagon by a cable that was strong enough to destroy any aircraft colliding with it. The balloons were intended to discourage dive-bombers and low level attacks, forcing pilots to fly higher into the range of concentrated anti-aircraft fire. By the middle of 1940 there were nearly 5,000 balloons over the London area. Although many found them a reassuring presence, they proved largely ineffective against the German high-level bombers.

Mary Slessor

For Christmas 1940, Miss Cornwall gave Audrey a book, which was to have a profound effect on her life and future. It was W. P. Livingstone's *Mary Slessor of Calabar*. In 1876 Mary Slessor had sailed for Nigeria, where she worked as a missionary almost without interruption until her death in 1915. Living among the people to whom she was called and becoming thoroughly conversant with the language, culture and customs, she managed to break down suspicion and fear, even among the most savage and powerful chiefs. She fought vigorously against witchcraft, drunkenness, twin-killing and other cruel practices; she set up churches, schools and hospitals all over her area of Africa and despite being crippled by arthritis in later years, refused to leave her post. She was instrumental in establishing trade between the coast and inland areas for the benefit of her people and in beginning the Hope Waddell Institution for training Africans in useful trades and medical work. She died in Calabar at the age of sixty-seven.

Audrey read Livingtone's book over and over again, so gripped was she by Mary's courage and spirit. With the stirrings of God in her heart, she prayed earnestly, 'Please, Lord, make me a missionary!' The seed was planted and although

Mary Slessor of Calabar

it was some time before she mentioned her desire to another Christian, her zeal for missionary work never waned from that moment.

Bombed

Audrey made friends with a couple of girls at Bourne & Hollingsworth. They were sisters and Christians, and they invited her to their home in Kent one weekend. While she was there a bomb hit the property next door and the vibrations were so strong that the plaster in her friends' house fell off the walls and the windows shattered, showering Audrey with glass; but she was unhurt.

In 1941, one of her friends, Valerie, from Bourne & Hollingsworth, resigned and went to work as a secretary at the Royal Bank of Scotland (RBS) in Bishopsgate. After a few months, she wrote Audrey a letter, in which she said, 'I don't know whether you would be interested, but here in the bank they are looking for girls to join the accounts department. Would you be interested? Just write and apply.' Audrey applied and was offered the job. She did not work at the front counter, but spent time on huge ledgers towards the back of the office. If a customer came in, especially if he was rich and important, he would go around the back to Audrey and her colleagues for an update on his account.

The bank had to keep essential businesses going and therefore its employees were in what was known as a 'reserved occupation' (also called 'essential services'), which was an occupation considered important enough to the country and the war effort to exempt those serving in it from military service, and it often prohibited them from enlisting on their own initiative. Examples of reserved occupations included medical practitioners and police officers. For Audrey, it meant she was never 'called up', nor could she leave the bank to take up a job elsewhere.

Having transferred to the Royal Bank of Scotland, Audrey had to find more suitable accommodation. She moved into a house in Endsleigh Gardens in the borough of Camden. Air raids took place usually at night and stations such as Euston (only a short distance to the northwest) and Paddington were prime targets for German bombers. On one never-to-be-forgotten night, the air raid siren's whine filled the air. Audrey and her companions hurried into the basement of their new home. Within minutes the house was hit by a bomb and collapsed, sending tonnes of rubble, twisted metal, wood and glass crashing down onto the basement's ceiling, which just managed to withstand the impact. Soot, which over the years had accumulated in the chimneys, enveloped the shelter and its occupants. Coughing and spluttering, and blackened like moles, they managed to crawl out through the destruction and into the clean air, thankful to be alive. The house and the basement were later demolished.

When things like this happened, Air Raid Precautions (ARP) wardens, mostly unpaid part-time volunteers, who patrolled the streets during air raids and doused incendiary bombs with sandbags, were on hand to rescue those injured or trapped because of the bombing. They were trained in fire fighting and first aid, and could keep an emergency situation under control until official help arrived. The ARP wardens directed Audrey and her friends to a place where they were given blankets and hot drinks.

The next day they went to Hyde Park Corner to a 'posh aristocratic house' where the Women's Voluntary Service (WVS), a women's organization set up to aid civilians, had a list of places where they could find a room or a bed. In the bombing of her home, Audrey lost all her possessions, except for the small number of belongings she had packed ready for when the siren sounded and she would have to dash to a shelter. She no longer had a home.

Westminster Chapel

Audrey had been attending St Paul's, Portman Square, when around April or May 1941 two girlfriends, who worked for the civil service, asked if she would like to accompany them one Sunday to Westminster Chapel, an evangelical stronghold. She readily agreed because it was such a joy to contemplate going to church with friends! Rev George Campbell Morgan was nearing the end of his second pastorate at the chapel (he retired in 1943) and Dr Martyn Lloyd-Jones, who had become the associate minister in 1939, was already well established. Morgan usually preached in the morning and Lloyd-Jones in the evening.

Audrey's first impressions of Westminster Chapel, built in the Lombardo style with a seating capacity of 2,500, never left her. That first Sunday morning, as she walked through the doors, the chapel's oval shape was the first thing to grab her attention, with first and second floor galleries set all the way round, and a suspended rostrum. A sense of excitement rose up inside her as she saw the place packed with so many young men and women.

The service began and everyone was quiet; only the organ could be heard. Then a distinguished looking gentleman, with winged collar, made his way to the rostrum. He began the service and everyone stood. They sang the first hymn and Audrey, who had never experienced anything quite like it, imagined she was in heaven! Then Campbell Morgan emerged. He preached from a verse in Micah: 'He hath showed thee, O man, what is good; and what doth the LORD require of thee, but to do justly, and to love mercy, and to walk humbly with thy God?' (Micah 6:8). Audrey was captivated. She had heard good preaching at St Paul's, but this was entirely different, on another level spiritually, and it was the first sermon that profoundly moved her. She came away that morning with a deeper sense of the majesty and awe of God.

Audrey heard Martyn Lloyd-Jones preach on many occasions. In her eyes he was not a very imposing figure as he stood in his black Geneva gown, collar and tie; but when he prayed, she was lifted into the heavenly places. 'He had such a wonderful way of explaining the word of God,' she enthused, 'and he preached with such logic, almost like a lawyer as he emphasized and re-emphasized the point he was making. After he died, I read his *Sermon on the Mount* series, and I could hear him again and see him standing in the rostrum. He was so earnest; he stressed not only the joy, but the seriousness of the Christian life.' Audrey never spoke to him, but she subsequently

G. Campbell Morgan

Martyn Lloyd-Jones

learned from others that he was a very warm man, who listened intently to what others had to say.

Church membership

Audrey managed to find a place to live in a hostel in Highbury Grove in the borough of Islington, where she struck up a friendship with a Christian girl, Barbara, who worked for the civil service. Sadly, because she was now living in North London, she found it too far to travel to Westminster Chapel on Sundays. Barbara's parents had asked three older, Victorian ladies, Rachel, Ruth and Phoebe Nunn, to keep an eye on their daughter during the war years. They were delightful, godly ladies, full of good works; they lived at The Angel, Islington, and attended Mount Zion Strict Baptist Chapel, Chadwell Street, Clerkenwell. When Barbara visited their home, usually on a Sunday, they also invited Audrey. Together they went to the chapel, which was how Audrey started to attend church regularly.

The area around Chadwell Street and The Angel was not very salubrious. One of the sisters, Rachel, took great interest in the 'better class' children who lived nearby and invited them to Sunday school. She asked Audrey if she would like to help with her class. Audrey was too reserved and shy and went only to observe. Eventually, when more confident, she taught the 'rougher' children at the chapel.

A hundred or so 'lovely Cockney people' attended the church, which was led by Pastor Robinson. A number of young people, who had not been called up, also attended, and they made Audrey feel most welcome. After Sunday morning at the chapel, they got together for afternoon tea, which by then had been rationed to two ounces per person per week. They studied the Bible and then returned for the evening service. In the summer, open-air meetings were held and, for the first time, Audrey was asked to share her testimony in public.

After she had been going to the church for a couple of months, the senior elder, Geoffrey Nunn (Justice of the Peace), a tall, thin, 'proper' gentleman, and the brother of the Nunn sisters, approached her. He took her into a little room and said,

'You have been coming to us for a number of weeks now and have made friends with the young people. Do you feel settled here and happy?'

'Oh yes,' she replied.

'Have you ever thought about membership?' he asked.

Audrey knew nothing about membership and looked puzzled.

'I hear you have been baptized,' inquired the elder. (At that time baptism by immersion, assent to the articles of the church, and approval by the members were the conditions of membership.) 'You should become a member of the church. Tell me your story.' Audrey shared her story, to which the senior elder replied, 'Go home and pray about it, and if you think it is right to come into membership, you will have to stand before the other elders and give your testimony again.' After seeking God, she decided to become a member. The elders deliberated over her decision and then for the third time she was asked to give her testimony before the whole church. There was a church meeting and Audrey was duly accepted. 'God, in his wisdom, bombed me out of my home to show me my need of membership!' said Audrey, with a wry smile on her face.

After some time, Audrey was invited to Mr and Mrs Nunn's house for prayer meetings, held in their home rather than at the chapel because of the severity of the air raids. The chapel was never bombed, but the area all around was destroyed. She found the Nunns 'very austere, but kind'.

The war

These were dark and destructive times in London in terms of the war and Audrey's life was often in danger. During the Blitz she learned to recognize the sound of enemy planes approaching and could hear the bombs exploding at ground level as she sat in her shelter. By the grace of God she had survived the Luftwaffe's devastating attack on London on 29 and 30 December 1940, when the Germans made extensive use of incendiary weapons.

She had also survived the 'savage climax' to the Blitz on 10 and 11 May 1941, when 507 German aircraft dropped 711 tonnes of bombs — including 86,173 incendiary bombs — on the city. By dawn London was near collapse and the morale of civilians severely shaken. More than 2,000 fires blackened the sky, 11,000 homes lay in ruins, the city's water mains were shattered, and more than 3,000 were dead or wounded. The House of Commons and St James's Palace were damaged, and hundreds of businesses were destroyed. Audrey did not know at the time, but that night was the last major raid on the city; the Blitz ended five days later.

At the end of that year Audrey heard that America and Britain had declared war on Japan, the day after the bombing of Pearl Harbour, and in January 1942 she realized that the first American forces had arrived on British soil; but additional soldiers did not ease her anxiety that England was about to be invaded. She knew Britain was a target, a fear that was highlighted as she watched 'dog fights' raging in the skies overhead. However, she did not know that the news was censored — the papers only reported that many German planes had been shot down. She never heard about troop ships being sunk, thousands of allies losing their lives on foreign battlefields or the mass murder of Jews by gassing at Auschwitz, which began in June 1942. She felt deeply the uncertainty of the times and was living under 'great strain'.

4
Days of preparation

Sharing her faith

During Audrey's days at Mount Zion Chapel, there was a small nucleus of young people at the church who were keen to take the gospel into the surrounding neighbourhood, which was a very deprived area. So they decided to go door knocking, which certainly was not easy after the bombing raids. They went two by two and prayed for an opportunity to speak about the Lord to those they met and to invite them to church. Most people were polite as they listened to these young, enthusiastic Christians, but not many responded positively.

Mount Zion had connections with St Mary's Islington, situated not far from St Paul's Cathedral and which was destroyed (except for the tower) in the Blitz. In the late 1940s a future archbishop of Sydney was vicar and described St Mary's as something of a 'cathedral of evangelicalism'. Both churches worked together to spread the good news of Christ. Audrey, who was now more confident to speak of her Saviour, made the most of opportunities that came her way. Over the next couple of years she was asked on several occasions to share her testimony at other Strict Baptist churches, such as Leyton, where the pastor, though beyond retirement age, had stayed on because the younger men had gone to fight in the war.

Audrey had a strong desire to learn more about the Bible and the teachings of Christ, so late on Saturday or Sunday nights after church she joined a group of like-minded people for Bible study. She was not aware of it at the time, but during these foundational years she was being grounded in the truth in preparation for a future on the mission field. At the studies, both old and young guided and encouraged her in the things of God, and she enthusiastically responded to their deep and sincere love for the Word of God and for the God of the Word.

A new home

Audrey's friend Valerie, with whom she had worked at Bourne & Hollingsworth and then followed to the Royal Bank of Scotland, lived with an older lady in a small flat in Hampstead, the Vale of Health. The Vale, with its village-like atmosphere, its listed buildings going back to the eighteenth century and its narrow streets, isolated on the heath, was a popular place to live, especially as it was only half an hour from the hustle and bustle of Piccadilly Circus. Audrey only saw Valerie occasionally at the bank as they worked in different departments, but one day Valerie approached her and said, 'I am going to work for a government department — the Ministry of Agriculture and Fisheries. My flatmate and I will be moving to Lochgilphead, Loch Fyne, Argyll. Would you like to live in our flat?'

Audrey was delighted and jumped at the invitation, especially as Valerie promised to leave all the furniture. Audrey moved as soon as Valerie left for Scotland (summer 1942). She particularly remembered coming out of Hampstead Underground station, the deepest London station, and climbing the steep hill to Hampstead Heath. Across the Heath were six large houses, in one of which was Audrey's little flat. From there it was easy to get to the bank on the Northern line.

At first she enjoyed living in the Vale, but there were disadvantages. It was a longer journey to get to Mount Zion and when winter came, her journey home was both difficult and dangerous through the blacked out London streets. She had to cross the Heath alone and one night a man followed her. She quickened her pace and managed to reach the safety of her flat before any harm was done. Sometimes on the Underground, she was the only lady among the passengers and felt intimidated and afraid.

Watford

While in London, Audrey found out where her mother was living and the sad news that her second husband had passed away. She plucked up the courage to go and see her. Her mother told her about a man named Cyril Hawker, who lived in Watford (thirty miles northwest of London). Cyril's wife had died unexpectedly, leaving two daughters, aged seven and ten. His unmarried sister had come to help out, but she was unwell; he was therefore looking for a housekeeper. Audrey's mother had applied for the job and was about to go for the interview when her daughter turned up. She asked Audrey to accompany her, which she did. Cyril owned a large house and was pleased for Audrey's mother to look after it. She lived in and before long fell in love with Cyril, a master builder and a churchgoer. They married and lived happily together.

A little while later, Audrey received a letter from her mother, who expressed concern that she was living on her own and travelling at night in such a dangerous part of the city. She kindly offered her a room in their large house. After thinking about it carefully, Audrey moved in with them and commuted to work each day.

Evidently Cyril also suggested to Audrey's mother, 'You have another daughter, whom you haven't seen for years — wouldn't you like her to visit?' Audrey's mother managed to contact her first husband, Mr Wells, with whom Valerie was still living; he brought Valerie to the station, where Audrey met her. Both sisters then lived with their mother, but Audrey only stayed for a short while. At the end of the 1940s, Valerie married and had three children.

Audrey was now living too far away to attend Mount Zion Chapel. On her last Sunday there, she was told that a letter had been sent to the church in Watford and the members would be looking out for her. The church was Watford (Strict) Baptist Tabernacle (now Derby Road Baptist Church), and the pastor was Rev George Bird.

'I want to be a missionary'

As mentioned earlier, when Audrey read the book *Mary Slessor of Calabar*, God planted a missionary seed in her heart. 'From that time on,' she said, 'I wanted to be a missionary in Africa. I read about Mary Slessor and how she went to Africa, just a funny little young lady, against all the odds, but she loved the Africans and got to know them and helped them and told them about Jesus Christ — her life and work just inspired me! That's what I wanted to do with my life. I wanted to go somewhere like that!'

She remembered the day when, from the top of Bourne & Hollingsworth, she had looked out of the window down onto Oxford Street and watched all the people going back and forth. 'No, not England,' she had cried in her heart. 'I want to go to Africa! Here in Great Britain there are Christian churches every hundred yards; it is a Christian country and everywhere there are churches people can attend, but in places like Africa, they have no knowledge of God and live wretched lives. I want to go to Africa!' She also remembered how, as a child, she always asked her mum to buy black dolls for her to play with — she never wanted to play with white dolls.

If she ever saw a missionary book — the bigger the volume the better in her mind — she saved her money until she could buy it. In this way she read about Hudson Taylor, David Brainerd, Adoniram Judson and many others. She loved reading about missions and how they were established, about other countries and their customs, and about the Christian church and its history. In fact, she could hardly stop reading, and the more she read the stronger grew her desire to be a missionary. All the dangers, discouragements and heartaches of the mission field only made her more determined to sacrifice all for Christ. Nothing was going to deter her from her goal.

Audrey went to Watford Tabernacle and on her first Sunday, as she left, Rev George Bird was standing on the steps saying goodbye to his congregation. Audrey held out her hand to greet him. The pastor looked her up and down and said, 'Where do you come from?' She told him and he replied, 'I have been waiting for you. It will be good if you can come to the prayer meeting in the week.'

After the prayer meeting a lady in her forties, Miss Evelyn Thompson, approached Audrey and welcomed her. She invited her back to Bushey, just outside Watford, where she lived with her elderly parents. Audrey went there several times for tea. On one of these occasions she asked Audrey to share about her life, at the conclusion of which Audrey cried out with a certain amount of passion, 'But I don't want to go on working at the bank, even though I am happy — I want to do something else. I want to be a missionary!' That was the first time Audrey had told anyone about her desire to serve God as a missionary.

Miss Thompson was quiet for a while, before replying, 'If the Lord has called you to be a missionary, you *will* be a missionary.' She then offered Audrey some wise advice, 'But don't run before his leading.' Audrey felt excited as she listened. Although she did not know Miss Thompson well, she somehow knew she was talking with someone who was acquainted with missionaries. Miss Thompson next asked, 'Why do you want to be a missionary? What has put that into your heart?' Audrey told her about Mary Slessor, after which Miss Thompson gently said, 'Continue to pray and the Lord will guide you.'

Miss Thompson then proceeded to tell Audrey about various significant events that had taken place in her own life. Some years ago the Lord had laid it on her heart to become a missionary. She went and studied at Mount Hermon, which was a ladies' missionary training college. (In the years before the war and after, there were theological colleges, but also specific missionary training colleges. Mount Hermon, Ridgelands Bible College and Redcliffe were the ladies' colleges; the men's missionary college was All Nations Bible College or ANBC, which had been founded in 1923 to replace Regions Beyond Missionary Union's Harley Missionary Training College, which had closed during World War I. ANBC was not able to function during World War II. Rev E. J. Poole-Connor, the founder of the Fellowship of Independent Evangelical Churches or FIEC, an association that regarded biblical truth as the only basis of

Christian fellowship, was largely responsible for its re-establishment, becoming its principal for three years. In 1970 Mount Hermon and Ridgelands merged with ANBC to become All Nations Christian College.)

Having studied at Mount Hermon for two years, Miss Thompson applied to Regions Beyond Missionary Union (RBMU). She went before the board and much to her delight was provisionally accepted, but she had to pass all her medicals to be a fully-fledged member. After the examinations it was announced, to her shock and horror, that because of fragile health, she was not suitable for work in the tropics. She was devastated and broken-hearted and had to return to secular work. At this point in her story she looked at Audrey and said with great seriousness and yet uncontrollable joy, 'Now I will tell you something. Ever since I received that terrible news, I have been praying that God would send someone in my place. What happened to me was not a mistake. When I met you, I felt *you were that person*! You must study the word of God for all you're worth, but do not go to the mission field unless you cannot possibly help it. Only go if that is the only thing you can do.'

Audrey was overcome with joyful anticipation as she listened to her friend. Was she going to follow in the footsteps of her heroine, Mary Slessor? Could she possibly become a missionary in Africa? Was her dream about to come true?

5
A missionary at last!

Soon after Miss Thompson's 'prophetic word', she wrote to the headquarters of RBMU, relating her conversation with Audrey and asking them to send her any literature that might be useful. Audrey came home from work one evening and found a large envelope waiting for her from the missionary union. She tore it open and read and re-read the magazines and pamphlets about missionary work in India and Africa. Her joy was indescribable! The accompanying letter from the secretary promised that RBMU would be praying for her and encouraged her to write to them if she needed any further help.

An informal interview

Without mentioning the desires of her heart to anyone else, she wrote to RBMU and told them why she felt God was calling her to be a missionary. Much to her delight, they invited her to Upper Norwood for an informal chat. She felt extremely nervous on the day of the interview. John Pritchard, pastor of Leigh Road Baptist Church, and Gordon Thomas, who later went to India as a missionary, were two members of the board, but only one of them interviewed Audrey. Audrey opened her heart to him. He endorsed what Evelyn had already told her, that she must be certain it was a call from the Lord, and not just youthful enthusiasm. 'You must settle down to study seriously the word of God at home in the evenings,' he advised. 'Do not leave your job, but prepare yourself to obey God's call.'

He passed several books to her, including *In Understanding Be Men*, a handbook of Christian doctrine by T. C. Hammond, and promised to send her questions on doctrine for her to answer each month, a bit like an in-house correspondence course. He would then be able to tell if she had understood the foundational truths of the Christian faith. He acknowledged that she was still very young, but gave the assurance that for the next year RBMU would be praying for her. Before the interview, Audrey had worried that she was already too old, so his words about her age were music to her ears! He told her to pray without ceasing, asking God to reveal his will to her.

Audrey was pleased to have a book to study and knew that if she were serious about becoming a missionary, the work would not be a burden to her. Before she left the room, the interviewer said that each Easter, RBMU held a conference at Slavanka Christian Hotel in Bournemouth, on the south coast of England. He suggested that if she was free and could afford it, she should write to the office and book a place.

First missionary conference

Audrey returned home elated at all that had happened and immediately started to plan for the conference. She was apprehensive about asking the bank for time off, especially as the holiday weekend, Good Friday to Easter Monday, was a difficult time, because in 1944 the end of the financial year fell at Easter and everyone was expected to work.

In fear and trepidation, and with many prayers shooting up to heaven, Audrey approached her boss Andrew Cunningham, a God-fearing, dour Scot, and asked for permission to take a few days off during that busy Easter weekend. 'No,' he immediately replied, 'that won't be possible.' Then after a slight pause, he asked, 'Anyway, what is it for?' Audrey told him. He looked at her and said gently, 'Well, my dear, you may go, but be very, very sure that what you have set your heart on, God wants you to do.' With joy in her heart and a lightness of step, Audrey hurried to book a place at the conference. She travelled on her own down to Bournemouth. Never before had she heard first-hand accounts of missionary work or met 'real live missionaries'.

Studying hard

Soon after the Bournemouth conference, Audrey's mother and stepfather moved away from Watford, and she went to live with another couple, fellow members of Watford Tabernacle. Audrey was also taken on as a fire fighter while working at the bank. As she was in a reserved occupation, the fire service recruited her and others to help them; so for one or two nights a week she had to be on hand, but she was never needed.

In the summer of 1944, Audrey was studying hard. One day at lunchtime she was out walking along Bishopsgate when she met a young Christian man, who told her about some lectures by well-known ministers, missionaries and business men that were being held each evening at St Andrews, Holborn. These men realized that with the end of the war approaching the need for theological training was paramount. Their ultimate vision was for an interdenominational, evangelical college that would counter the rising tide of liberal scholarship in western universities and prepare Christians to interact with their post-war world. (Their vision was realized in London Bible College, now London School of Theology.) Audrey attended these lectures for three hours every evening, after which Rev W. J. Aldis and Rev Russell-Bowden signed her certificate to confirm that she had completed the course.

That autumn Audrey wrote to her mentor at RBMU to inform him that she was attending the lectures and that she was finding it difficult to do any additional study. He was delighted about the lectures and told her not to worry about the correspondence course. Once again Audrey, just an 'ordinary person' by her own admission, could see that God was working all things out 'after the counsel of his own will'.

A second interview

About February or March 1945, Audrey had completed the year recommended by RBMU and was therefore able to apply again. She had no doubts about her future, and the desire to be a missionary in Africa was as strong as ever. In response to her letter of application, she received a reply, which included a great deal of literature and a long questionnaire, at the end of which she was asked: 'Are you single? Are you married? Are you engaged to be married? Are you likely to be engaged to be married?' Audrey was of course single and unengaged. In fact, she was determined, perhaps influenced by her parents' difficult relationship, *never* to get married.

RBMU replied, asking her to meet the board of directors for a formal interview at the mission's base, Homelands in Upper Norwood. With nervousness bordering on fear, Audrey entered the large house, with many rooms and set in its own grounds. In the boardroom were eight or nine 'august gentlemen'. They sat around a table and each one asked Audrey well-prepared questions, including questions about her theological and doctrinal beliefs. They asked about her background, how she became a Christian, about her personality and temperament, and naturally, why she felt the Lord was calling her to be a missionary. The interview lasted an hour or more. Audrey found it 'nerve-racking' and 'an awesome experience'.

When it was over, she was ushered into a side room to wait while the directors deliberated about whether or not she had really received a call from the Lord. About forty-five minutes later, she was called back into the boardroom. She held her breath. 'We have accepted you as a missionary to Congo,' announced the spokesman. Audrey was quite overwhelmed — a sense of excitement and dread seemed to collide in her heart. Her passion was for Africa and RBMU's field was Congo, so it was only natural that she was officially accepted as a Congo missionary.

At this time the war was still in progress and nobody was sure when it was going to end, so the board cautioned their new missionary, saying that she would need to go to a missionary college, but her training would have to be put on hold until she was released from her reserved occupation with the bank.

Redcliffe

RBMU's secretary, Ebenezer G. Vine, an English Baptist pastor, had joined the board in 1939. A year later he gave up a successful business to devote his time to missions, and in 1942

Ebenezer G. Vine

he was appointed General Secretary of the Mission. 'His genial presence and loving personality warmed and cheered headquarters during the final dreary years of war ... It may be said of him that he had "to his God a heart of flame; to others a heart of love; to himself a heart of steel". Because he was completely unselfconscious, he could listen to others as if nothing else mattered in the world.'

So heavy was his missionary burden that in 1948 he represented the needs of the British mission in North America. He only expected to remain there three months, but in fact stayed fifteen years, not only launching RBMU's work in the United States and Canada, but also beginning its extensive ministries in Indonesia. Vine went to speak with Audrey more informally after the interview and advised her to apply to Redcliffe Missionary Training College.

Back in Victorian times, there were no missionary training facilities for women and mission agencies were reluctant to accept single women who had not been 'tested' by the trials of life. Then in 1892 Mrs Tottenham, a godly and resolute lady with a passion for missions, set up the YWCA Testing and Training Home in London with 'twelve candidates, two ladies and a cook'. Taking an innovative and radical approach to mission training, Mrs Tottenham offered a unique blend of practical subjects such as first aid and carpentry, alongside the more traditional subjects of church history and the life of Christ, to prepare candidates for cross-cultural ministry. Many onlookers were sceptical at first, but the new centre, which became known as Redcliffe Missionary Training College, flourished. During her lifetime, Mrs Tottenham saw hundreds of women serving God as missionaries in many different countries.

Audrey wrote to Redcliffe, asking if she could become a student as soon as she was released from the bank. The college agreed and she started training in September 1945. In the time between her application to Redcliffe and her first day, she met a man who was going to have a profound influence on her future life.

6
Elleea

During Easter 1945, the RBMU annual spring conference was again held at Slavanka in Bournemouth. With great enthusiasm Audrey set off on her own to the south coast. On this occasion a group of missionaries, who had arrived home from Congo the previous autumn on furlough, were the speakers. Audrey listened intently to what the missionaries said, while at the same time remembering all that had happened to her since the previous conference.

Talking with missionaries

There was a couple there from Congo, Mr and Mrs Alfred Ivimey, who were sitting with 'a nervous' Audrey at the lunch table. They had a kindly manner and asked Audrey, 'Are you interested in missionary work?'

'Yes I am,' replied Audrey, with unbounded excitement in her voice.

'Do you think that perhaps one day you will be a missionary — in Congo?'

Audrey could hardly believe what she was hearing and the word Congo almost made her jump with anticipation. 'I hope so!' she replied.

There was another missionary, Lawrence Walling (his wife was not with him), who spoke with Audrey and the two of them discovered they were both from Leigh-on-Sea, which immediately calmed Audrey's nerves and gave them a good starting point for conversation. Walling told her all about his work in Congo. There was another young man, Elleea Featherstone, whom Audrey heard speak at the conference, but she had no private conversation with him and had not thought any more highly of him than any of the others.

Falling in love

By the end of 1933, Elleea Featherstone had completed his first term in Congo, and returned on furlough from a second term in 1938. When the war broke out, he was back in Congo, trapped along with the other missionaries, who could not find a way home because the boats and ships on which they would normally have travelled had been commandeered by respective governments to carry troops. He did not return to his Cheltenham home until the autumn of 1944 when around six to eight missionaries managed to get a passage on a ship, which had to sail in convoy to circumvent the Germans. This increased considerably the length of their journey, so when Audrey heard him speak in Bournemouth he was in the middle of his year-long furlough.

After the conference Audrey had to travel back to London to be at work the following morning. In the war years, trains were not all that frequent and were packed with passengers, making it almost impossible to get a seat unless you arrived early. Audrey left Slavanka and made her way to Boscombe Station, where there were hundreds of people milling around. She walked along the platform looking through the compartment windows to see if there were any empty seats. Suddenly someone called her name. She turned round and there was Elleea Featherstone standing at a carriage door. He said politely, 'I knew the train would be full and so I came down early to reserve a seat for you.' Audrey was taken aback by his kindness, thanked him and waved him goodbye, but thought no more of it as the train sped back to London.

A day or so later, she received a letter, which read, 'Dear Audrey, I hope you got home all right. I am just writing to you because I would like to know whether you are phone-able or see-able? Elleea.'

Audrey was obviously surprised and could only conclude that the Ivimeys, and perhaps others, had mentioned to him the burden she had for Congo. She wrote back a short reply and said, 'Yes, I am see-able,' and told him where she worked. Elleea had been staying at Homelands, but after the Bournemouth conference he went back with the Ivimeys to their home in Kent. Two or three days later he returned to Homelands. Later Audrey received a large parcel from him through the post. She ripped off the brown paper and lifted the lid of the box, which was filled with tissue paper and cotton wool, in the middle of which was a bunch of beautiful violets and primroses, which Elleea had picked in Kent. A day or so later, he unexpectedly turned up outside the bank when she left work, a surprise he repeated several times over the next few weeks. Together they walked in the West End and in St James's Park, and went rowing on the lake there — all the time talking about Congo.

In May each year the various missionary societies held large meetings in London, which they called 'The May Meetings'. On one particular Saturday afternoon in May, RBMU conducted afternoon and evening meetings, which Audrey attended. Elleea was one of the speakers. When the tea interval arrived, because it was wartime, everyone went off to the nearest café, as it was not possible to organize tea at the venue. Elleea waited for Audrey and arm in arm they ambled along Victoria Street. Suddenly they saw two or three RBMU directors coming towards them. These stern-looking gentlemen stared at them closely and then walked on without saying a word. Audrey felt embarrassed as she remembered her answers to the questionnaire, when she had assured RBMU that she had no intention of getting married. When Elleea got back to Homelands he lost no time in telling Ebenezer Vine about their relationship. Vine was delighted.

Engaged

On 7 May 1945, the German forces unconditionally surrendered to the Allies. Audrey stood with Elleea in front of the Mansion House as everyone came out of their offices for the celebrations. Field Marshall Montgomery, who had accepted the formal surrender of the German military at Luneburg Heath on 4 May, addressed the great crowd to confirm that the war was over. He publicly gave thanks to God.

In the summer of 1945 Audrey was still working in the bank, but was able to see Elleea whenever he was on deputation work in London. One summer's evening in St James's Park they went rowing on the lake. All of a sudden Elleea produced an engagement ring and asked for Audrey's hand in marriage. Audrey accepted without a moment's hesitation. Among family and close friends, Elleea became known as Larry, because he was as gentle as a lamb.

Days at Redcliffe

In August, Audrey left the bank, which was being restructured as men returned from the war and wanted their old jobs back. The following month she started her two years' training at Redcliffe, then situated in Chiswick by the river. She had to save every penny to pay for her college fees. The course was residential, but a kind elderly couple in Watford allowed her to stay at their home during holiday periods so she always had somewhere to go.

Redcliffe brought Audrey down to earth with a bump from the heavenly joy she was experiencing over her engagement, for the college was *very* strict. During the war it only had five or six students, but afterwards an influx of about fifteen to twenty new students arrived on the scene. Miss Nash, the principal, called the new intake 'the invasion'. They were all young people who had grown up in the war, and to go to the restrictive regime of college life was, in Audrey's words, 'a bit of a shock to the system'.

The students represented many different missionary societies and fields, and some had not even applied or been accepted by a mission when they joined the college. Two or three shared a room. If Miss Nash reckoned two girls might *not* enjoy each other's company, she deliberately put them together. The reasoning behind her actions was because, on the mission field, you could not pick and choose with whom you worked — you might have to work with someone particularly irksome to your natural temperament.

During Audrey's first term she was put with a woman called Florence Stebbing, who was going out to the mission field with WEC International (Worldwide Evangelization for Christ), and also a small Irish girl. In the evening, when it was time for bed, Florence, in an authoritative but respectful tone, said, 'On your knees, girls,' because the students were expected to have an hour's devotional time. When that was over, she ordered, 'Now into bed, girls.' Despite her rather bossy nature, Florence was both well liked and esteemed.

At 6:30 a.m. the bell rang and after a cold wash, the students prayed and read the Bible for an hour before doing chores such as cleaning and cooking. At meal times they sat at three long tables and were not allowed to pass by any food they did not like — all had to be eaten. Audrey hated the skin on custard and if it happened to fall onto her pudding while the custard was being poured, she had to eat it. Again it was useful training because on the mission field there were few delicacies to enjoy and little food could be rejected. After Audrey left college, she appreciated the training, but at the time she was not so sure!

In November 1945, Elleea returned to the field. Audrey asked the formidable Miss Nash if she could have the afternoon off to attend the valedictory meeting that had been arranged for him and others at Homelands. Generally speaking, Redcliffe did not approve of engaged couples; they thought such relationships were unnecessary distractions to important preparation and study, but the mission did support Elleea and Audrey. So Elleea returned to Congo and Audrey continued at Redcliffe. She missed him terribly, especially on Saturdays when they usually spent time together.

Leaving Redcliffe

After her first year Audrey stayed at Homelands for the holidays. Ebenezer Vine asked to see her because RBMU wanted Elleea's furlough, which occurred after four years, to coincide with Audrey's, which, as a new missionary, occurred after three years. Furloughs in those days were pretty inflexible in order to accommodate missionary colleagues. Mr Vine told Audrey that for the two furloughs to coincide she must go to the field at the end of 1946. In an unprecedented step, he assured her of RBMU's view, that because she had done a fair bit of Bible Study already, she could end her studies at Redcliffe after just one year. He promised to write to Miss Nash and explain the situation.

Predictably Miss Nash was not supportive. She called Audrey in and gave her a long lecture, saying, 'I am not happy about this, Audrey. I feel I am sending you out half-baked!' By now Audrey had experienced several 'chats' with Miss Nash, for every term students were summoned into her office for what was a 'pretty uncomfortable time'. She was a spiritual and discerning lady, who pinpointed weaknesses and defects in character that might be a hindrance on the mission field. Audrey found her insight 'intimidating, but helpful', and was thankful for it. Reluctantly, Miss Nash agreed to Vine's recommendation; so Audrey's studies concluded at Redcliffe in the summer of 1946 after only one year.

7
To Africa

Visitations

When Audrey was interviewed by RBMU, Gordon Guinness was the chairman of the mission, but soon afterwards he was succeeded by the minister of Rye Lane, Peckham, Rev Theo Bamber. In the summer of 1946 Audrey was living at Homelands undergoing more training when Bamber asked her to do 'deaconess work' at Rye Lane, which involved visiting some of his parishioners, and then writing a report on each person she had seen.

Generally people were kind to her as she turned up on their doorsteps, and she benefited spiritually from the work, but she still lacked confidence and felt as if she did not belong anywhere. In her mind she had no 'accomplishments' or gifts — a diffidence that remained with her for the rest of her life, particularly when she was in England. Interestingly, when she was on the field in Congo her God-given abilities came to the fore, along with a boldness to work for the kingdom of Christ.

She continued her visitation work into the autumn, while assembling together everything she needed for Congo. She had been given a long list of necessities to buy, with only a few coupons: cotton dresses, sandals, a mosquito net and so on, items that had to last for three years. Accommodation and food were provided by Homelands and she went everywhere on her bike to save money. The important lessons she had learned at Redcliffe about frugality were put to good use, for RBMU wanted their missionaries to live by faith and the board made it clear that nothing was guaranteed: 'If we have funds, you will have an allowance; if we have no funds, you will not have an allowance.'

Antwerp

By the end of September 1946 Audrey was ready to leave for Congo as soon as she could arrange a suitable passage. The war had come to an end, which meant that ships were free to sail again, but it was still not easy for anyone to get anywhere. About the same time a senior missionary couple, Len and Mabel Hanson, 'wonderful linguists', were waiting to return to Congo and the RBMU board decided that Audrey should leave with them. All three needed to travel to Antwerp first as Congo was a Belgian colony. If a ship docked, they could then commence their journey, along with many other colonial people.

Early in November, Mr and Mrs Hanson and Audrey arrived at Liverpool Street station, with friends who had come to see them off. They travelled on to Harwich and boarded the ferry to Antwerp.

Audrey was excited about the prospect of missionary work in Congo, but her feelings for Elleea, after a twelve month separation, had cooled. Initially, when he had returned to Congo, she had missed him terribly. At that time her love was strong and vibrant, but as the months went by and she adjusted to being on her own, life without him became more bearable. She had only been going out with him for a few months before he left for Congo, so her uncertainty was understandable. Elleea, on the other hand, was deeply in love with Audrey, as his 'beautiful letters and drawings' to her demonstrated.

Audrey, Len and Mabel arrived in Antwerp near to Christmas. It was extremely cold and snowing when they docked. After a few days, the Hansons managed to get a berth on a ship called *Copacabana,* but there was no room for Audrey, so she was left behind on her own in a foreign city. She stayed in the *pension* (European boarding house) of a Belgian lady, who owned a large house and often took in missionaries, either doctors and nurses or educationalists. There were about nine others in the house, men and women of different nationalities, and Audrey was the only person from the UK.

Mr and Mrs Hanson with their granddaughter Angela

Each day for the next week or two Audrey made the cold and lonely journey along the snow covered streets, with icicles hanging from the buildings, to the dock to see if there was a ship that could take her to Africa. After the privations of war torn Britain, she was amazed at the abundance of food in Belgian shops. On one of her journeys she stepped inside Antwerp Cathedral during mass, and was amused by all the people going to church to receive a 'blessing', and by the ladies in their pretty aprons asking for an offering!

The journey to Congo

At last a passenger/cargo ship called the *Mar del Plata* docked and Audrey was given a sailing date. On that day, with heavy snow still falling, she excitedly and nervously walked up the gangway onto the ship, which carried about 100 passengers. Holding all her possessions in two tin trunks, she was told the number of her cabin. When she opened the door she immediately recoiled at the sight of cockroaches all over the walls, floor and ceiling! As she sat on her bed, with a strong desire to serve the Lord, she wondered what exactly life would be like in Africa. She knew there were tough times ahead and she recalled the words of a senior missionary, 'You are still quite young, but that is an advantage; for when you go to the mission field in your early twenties and you face difficulties, like learning a language, you can make the most terrible mistakes, and just laugh at yourself. When older people go out, it is not so easy for them. Don't worry, you will adapt. Always keep the Lord Jesus at the centre of your life.' And that is just what Audrey intended to do.

The ship left Antwerp via the Scheldt Estuary, and sailed out into the North Sea and south to the Bay of Biscay. The first port of call was Tenerife, where the captain docked for a day or two to pick up fresh produce. After an uneventful two week journey, the *Mar del Plata* sailed past the mouth of the Congo River, down to Lobito on the Angolan coast, where ships usually travelled before heading back north to Congo, which took another three or four days. They entered the mouth of the Congo River and travelled some twenty miles to Matadi, the main port into Congo.

In places the Congo River, the largest river in Western Central Africa, with an overall length of 2,734 miles, is three to four miles wide, with over 4,000 islands within its banks, more than fifty of which are at least ten miles in length. It has been estimated that almost 400 kilometres of the Congo are unnavigable due to these islands plus a number of cataracts, in particular at Livingstone Falls. The river and its tributaries, both of which have figured prominently in the region's history, flow through the second largest rain forest in the world, and serve as a main artery for transportation into the African interior.

With the sights and sounds of the huge Congo River before her, Audrey docked at Matadi, where there was great excitement as people rushed on board to greet family and friends. Everyone eventually disembarked, but Audrey was left alone on deck, overlooking the quay. She did not know what to do next. Then she noticed a man pushing his way through the crowds and making his way up the gangway. 'Are you Miss Wells?' he asked excitedly. 'I have had word of your coming.' Audrey was *very* pleased to see him. His name was Mr Ornhamann, and he was general secretary of the Swedish Mission at Matadi. He helped Audrey through customs and took her back to his bungalow, where his wife was waiting to cook their guest something to eat. They told Audrey that they would make arrangements for her to travel by train on the next phase of her journey.

The following day she boarded a wood-fuelled train which, after it had travelled many miles, stopped to take on more wood. At times Audrey was quite nervous as the train crossed narrow ledges high up in mountainous and rocky areas, with the Congo River a long way below. All along the route were mission posts and whenever the train stopped, children ran to greet the passengers singing the carols they had learned. Audrey recognized the tunes, but the language was still a mystery to her.

About twelve hours later she arrived in Leopoldville (renamed Kinshasa in 1966). She jumped off the train, looked around and again thought to herself, 'Now what do I do?'

Union Mission Hostel, Leopoldville

Before long a Congolese gentleman, Mr Lutete, approached her and spoke to her in French. He had been sent by RBMU. He was the manager of the Union Mission Hostel (UMH), which was a lodging house for missionaries coming from the interior. He took charge of Audrey and drove her in his car to the hostel, where she was given a small room with one or two others. As Audrey sat in the lounge, watching the lizards scuttling here and there, she thanked God for watching over her thus far on what had been a long, tiring, but exciting journey to Congo, her home for the next twenty-five years.

8
The journey continues

On to Coquilhatville

The following morning, someone came into the UMH and Audrey heard him asking after her. The Baptist Missionary Society worked in Leopoldville and this gentleman, Mr Reynolds, worked for the mission along the river. He invited Audrey back for coffee to his bungalow overlooking Stanley Pool, a lake-like expansion in the lower reaches of the Congo River about thirty-five kilometres long and twenty-three kilometres wide, with Bamu Island at its western end. The Pool, named after Henry M. Stanley, the explorer, who was also known in Congo as *Bula Matari* (Breaker of Rocks), is the beginning of the navigable part of the Congo River; just below it the river descends hundreds of metres in a series of rapids known as the Livingstone Falls.

When Audrey arrived, Mrs Reynolds was in the middle of packing for the trip home. The couple were very kind to Audrey, who came to regard them 'like parents'. They gave her good counsel about life in Congo and agreed to make arrangements for the journey to her final destination — 1,000 miles further on!

Once a month a large riverboat sailed from Leopoldville all the way around to Stanleyville, which had been founded by the explorer Stanley in 1883, but the Reynolds were not happy for Audrey to travel alone on this boat; so they made some phone calls and discovered that there was a small plane going as far as Coquilhatville (now Mbandaka), the town hall of which was only about five miles north of the geographic equator line. Audrey got up early the next morning and Lutete took her to the airfield. After meeting the pilot, co-pilot and another gentleman, they took off. Audrey gazed out of the window at the deep Congo tributaries meandering their way through dense forest. Occasionally she saw spirals of smoke drifting through the trees from the tribal villages, although she never saw the villages themselves.

They arrived at Coquilhatville and touched down on a muddy landing strip sometime between 11:00 a.m. and midday in the blazing heat of the equator. The four of them scrambled out of the plane and after the pilot and co-pilot had sorted out their cargo, those two left. Audrey stood by the other passenger, an American, with whom she had exchanged pleasantries. He was a representative for his firm 'Coats', the cotton traders.

After about twenty minutes a truck rumbled along and the American asked the driver if they could have a lift into town. They jumped in the back and were eventually dropped outside a provisions store, which looked like a ramshackle building from an old Western film. Once inside the store, they asked a buxom Belgian lady if they could both have a room for the night and something to eat. The American was given a room, but the lady told Audrey to wait while she contacted the mission, which was about five miles out of Coquilhatville. The mission comprised a large educational establishment that was run by an American organization called 'The Disciples of Christ', a denomination of Christian Protestantism founded by Thomas Campbell, Alexander Campbell and Barton W. Stone that had grown out of the Restoration Movement. The lady returned from making the phone call with a big smile on her face and announced that on account of a retreat, there was only one missionary there, but she would come from Bolenge to meet Audrey. This lady and her husband had been senior missionaries with 'The Disciples of Christ', but about a year or so previously her husband had been killed in a motorbike accident. Grief-stricken, his wife had travelled home, only to return to the field some time later. Audrey rode with her by truck along bumpy mud roads to Bolenge.

Mission stations along the way

Audrey was advised to take some food along with her for the next stage of her journey, so she returned to the buxom lady at the provisions store to buy all she needed. She then looked out for a boat that would take her to the Congo Balolo Mission. A couple of days later she boarded a paddle steamer, captained by a Congolese man. The steamer had one or two dirty cabins on the upper deck and as it sailed it pushed along six or eight barges covered with iron and containing sacks of flour, sugar, palm oil and other necessities, two in front and the rest at the side. The barges and the lower deck of the steamer were crammed with Congolese, with their goats and chickens.

Audrey travelled for four or five long days up the Lulonga River, sailing against the current. She was the only white person on board; it was very noisy and she could not understand anything anyone said. She was glad to have a cabin to herself, but at night she felt nervous and uneasy, as there was no way of locking it. She therefore put one of her tin trunks up against the door. Once or twice the steamer stopped to take on extra wood. After two or three days it pulled into a beach and high up on the cliff Audrey saw Lulonga mission station. About once a month the steamer delivered letters and the two missionary ladies from the station came to collect them. On seeing Audrey they invited her back to the mission station for a meal.

The next day they called at Bosodjafo mission station, arriving in the afternoon, and Audrey was delighted to meet up with the Ivimeys once again. Lillian Ivimey was very fond of cats and during the evening meal she saw nothing wrong with her cat jumping on the table and licking up Audrey's custard!

Audrey moved on to a third mission station, Ikau (the mission stations were usually about 120 miles apart). At about one o'clock in the morning she awoke to the sound of the ship's hooter, which sounded day or night as a 'wake up' call to the missionaries at the station to come and collect their letters. She slipped out of bed, pulled her trunk away from the door and looked towards the shore. All she could see was a steep cliff face. She heard voices calling, 'Please come and pick up the letters and this woman.' She noticed another boat moored between the steamer and the cliff face. It was *The Livingstone*, which had been originally sent out by Britain in 1818 in eighty different boxes and transported by Congolese to Stanley Pool, where it took 16,000 rivets to put it back together again!

As Audrey disembarked, she was overwhelmed by the sounds of the night — the noisy cicadas, frogs croaking, night birds singing, and the beautiful scent from the forest. Ross and Christine Manning were pastoral workers, and at the time of Audrey's arrival Ross was away in the district working, so Christine escorted her back to the house and made her a 'disgusting cup of tea', Congolese style. (It was several months before Audrey could stomach Congolese tea.) She crawled into bed at about 2:00 a.m. exhausted, but happy she had arrived safely at Ikau.

Back in the UK, RBMU did not make decisions concerning the area of work in which an outgoing missionary was to be involved. Instead, a yearly field conference was held for ministry and discussion, and 'the big headache' was always staffing the mission stations, which were situated all along the river where they could be easily reached by boat. These field conferences were usually held in Ikau. During the last field conference, before Audrey had arrived, it was decided she needed to go to Baringa for language study.

Baringa

She waited for Ross to return and he drove her to the next mission station at Baringa, some 100 miles to the west and where medical, church and educational work were proceeding unhindered. Crossing some of the rivers was a dangerous exercise, sometimes with only logs or tree trunks to keep the wheels on track. The mission station at Baringa, set three or four miles into the forest, included a large mission hospital, where up to a thousand lepers from a nearby settlement received treatment.

There was also a school for boys, who did not start their education until the age of nine or ten (at that time there was no schooling for girls), and a training centre, part evangelistic, part schooling, for young men who wanted to become 'village teachers'. Their training lasted for two years at the mission station, after which they gathered people together for ministry.

Meeting Elleea again

On her first day at Baringa, Arthur and Elizabeth Wright and Mr and Mrs Campbell decided that as a paddle steamer was due to come up the Baringa River, Audrey should be put on that boat to travel to Mompono, where she could meet up with Elleea. When the steamer arrived, Audrey boarded and after a two or three hour wait set off up river. As the boat left, Audrey was facing the shore, waving goodbye to her new missionary friends. Consequently she did not notice another boat that was sailing down river.

Suddenly the four missionaries on the shore started shouting frantically at the captain in Lomongo, the language of the Mongo people, trying to get him to stop midstream because there was a 'white man' on the other boat who wanted to meet the 'white woman' on his boat! At first Audrey could not understand what all the fuss was about, but then she turned and saw Elleea on the other boat. Apparently he had gone to the captain to ask him to manoeuvre his boat alongside the boat that had just left the shore. Although there was a strong current, the captains managed to stop their boats midstream and Elleea, whom Audrey had not seen for fifteen months, was able to clamber over the barges and onto Audrey's boat. By this time a large crowd had gathered to see what all the commotion was about, but Elleea took Audrey into the quiet of one of the cabins — and so they were reunited. It was St Valentine's Day 1947.

They spent a few happy days together in Mompono, where Audrey was able to renew her contact with the Hansons, whom she had not seen since they had left Antwerp. She then took the courier boat, packed with hundreds of Africans, back to Baringa.

Audrey stayed at Baringa for about four months for language study, until the middle of June, and during that time she was struck by the peacefulness of Congo, in contrast to the horrors of the war she had lived through. Dr Arthur Wright, who served as a doctor at the hospital, along with his wife, Elizabeth, initially helped Audrey with her language lessons, but he was so busy with medical work that it was not easy to maintain any consistency. Mr and Mrs Campbell were another missionary couple at Baringa, and Audrey soon got to know them. With her grammar book and dictionary in hand she often accompanied Ella Campbell on her afternoon visits among the tribeswomen, in the hope of learning more about the language.

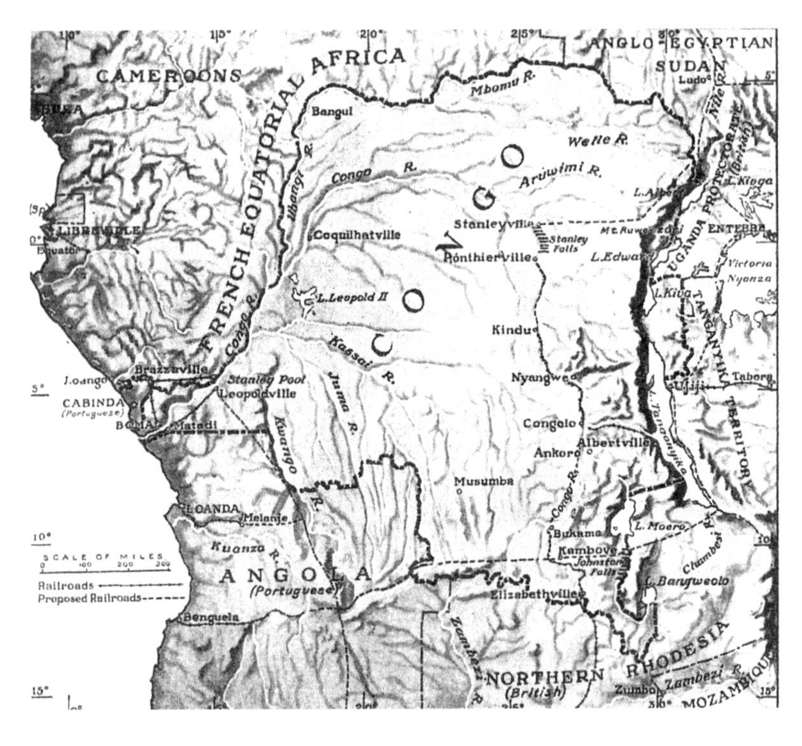

Map of the Congo Basin in West and Central Africa

9
Life in the Congo Basin

The Congo Basin forest covers more than one million square miles, an area twice the size of France, and contains over 10,000 species of plants, 1,000 species of birds, and 400 species of mammals. It is also home to millions of people, many of whom depend on the forest for their livelihoods.

A Congo house

The houses Audrey visited were built on brick piles because the pioneer missionaries thought that malaria, for centuries linked with poisonous vapours of swamps or stagnant water, came up from the ground. The living area, divided into three, was reached after climbing a few steps. There were windows covered with wire mesh and a veranda was usually built all around the house. For hygiene reasons the toilet, just a deep hole in the ground with a pile of sand nearby, was situated about 200 metres away, which was not much fun if needed in the night, especially as the area was infested with cockroaches.

It never rained in Congo without a heavy thunderstorm, which, from Audrey's home, moved upriver, from the east. These storms, lasting three or four hours, occurred in spring and again from September to early December, usually late in the afternoon, and were sparked off by the intense heat. The Africans said, '*Wane wa mbula*', meaning 'heat and rain'. As the storm intensified, thatched roofs were torn apart and rain poured into the houses. Audrey remembered placing bowls and buckets everywhere to catch the water. After the storm passed, it continued to rain for two or three more hours. The rainy season was over before Christmas, enabling the missionaries to arrange special outdoor meetings during that festive period.

There was no electricity or running water, so large kerosene containers were placed under the joint in the roof to catch the rainwater, which was then boiled. Baths were made up of part cold water and part 'smoky water'. Each house had a kitchen with an iron stove called a 'modern mistress', one side of which was for a fire, the other for an oven. Schoolboys collected the firewood, but some of it was too wet or rotten to burn properly. The missionaries baked their own bread from flour that was ordered down river, which was only fit for consumption once the weevils and maggots had been sieved out.

Food

Manioch, a white, stringy, bitter-tasting root vegetable, which takes nearly a year to grow to a suitable size, was the staple food of the area. The women planted it, tended it all the time and then gathered it into conical baskets, which they carried on their backs. It was extremely heavy, and Audrey saw them trudging along the forest paths in the equatorial heat to the nearest stream, where they soaked it to remove the prussic acid. They then beat out the water, steamed it and kneaded it into a long sausage shape. They also used the manioch leaf, pounding it to a pulp. When it was bright red, they added palm oil and peppers/chillies, making a delicious meal.

Some of the Congolese tribes were still cannibals, while others hunted monkeys, boasting that monkey meat was the next best thing to human flesh. Large rats were often found up in the roofs of houses and the locals enjoyed rat stew. Sometimes the missionaries watched as the Congolese put their ears to rotting tree stumps, which they somehow knew contained large white translucent maggots, which they ate alive. In August, caterpillars were evident. These were cooked and eaten with delight, even though they turned the tribesmen's mouths black and gave them a bad stomach-ache. Flying ants were attracted to the hot hurricane lamps, which burned off their wings. The Africans then scooped them off the floor and cooked them. The forest fruits were not indigenous, but had been largely brought from South America centuries before.

Wild animals

Along the riverbanks were many fallen trees, and crocodiles, difficult to see, lazed in the tropical heat. The Congo River was full of them. If a mother went to the riverside with a child and her attention was distracted for only a few seconds, it presented an opportunity for a crocodile to strike and drag the child underwater and back to its lair. Many mothers lost a child in this way. When travelling by canoe, the missionaries not only paddled close to the bank to avoid the strong currents, but also kept a careful watch for crocodiles.

Hippos also lived in the river, and they could easily capsize a boat and drown its occupants. Leopards frequently attacked chicken houses, but a flashlight shone in their eyes was usually enough to frighten them away. Once a leopard confronted Audrey, but thankfully as soon as she turned on her flashlight it fled. Monkeys and chimps were also prevalent and elephants were pests. Hundreds of them lived in the forest. They were aggressive, especially if they had babies with them, and could easily overturn a truck. If one approached, it was best not to move. At night they trampled the manioch gardens of the villagers, who stayed up all night beating their drums in an attempt to drive them away. The elephants also searched for anything that was edible in the mission stations, where the missionaries sat in the doorways of their mud huts, watching them eat the fruits of the forest. A fire was usually enough to make them keep their distance.

Once, later, during the Simba uprising (see chapter 16), Audrey and Elleea were in bed when they heard a rustling sound outside their hut. They thought it was the Simbas who had come to murder them. Elleea quietly jumped out of bed and shone his flashlight into the forest. With a sigh of relief he called Audrey to take a look at a group of elephants feeding. Suddenly the elephants were startled by the light and made a hasty retreat, but a large anthill blocked their path. The leading elephant charged at the anthill, only to slide to the ground as he tried to climb over it. This happened several times before the herd managed to make good its escape. Both Audrey and Elleea thought the scene was hilarious.

On another occasion, when cycling through the thick forest from the Baringa hospital station to her home in the *lifeta* (the leper camp), Audrey cycled straight into a herd of elephants; they could easily have trampled her to death, especially if they had had their young with them. They were only about 100 metres away. Audrey stopped, pulled to the side of the road and crouched quietly down. Thankfully they did not see her, but crossed the path and went on their way into the forest.

Once a village pastor had a miraculous escape. At a turn in the path, he fell off his bike right in the way of a herd of elephants. He stayed perfectly still, anticipating imminent death, but amazingly not one of the elephants stepped on him as they passed by! God preserved his life.

Birds, snakes and insects

Living in the trees were birds of all kinds, the most popular being the Congo African grey parrot, with light grey feathers, a cherry red tail and a black beak. It was about thirty centimetres long and a 'good talker'. Hawks, circling above, swooped down and attacked chicks, while poisonous snakes of all kinds were particularly fond of basking on the thatched roofs.

From early on, snakes were one of Audrey's greatest fears, but she learned to cope with them. On one occasion she pulled a book from the shelf and there was a snake staring at her! Fortunately it did not strike. She never killed the snakes, just stepped aside and let them slither by. In all her years in the Congo a snake never bit her, but on many occasions a scorpion stung her and the infected area became very swollen. One afternoon she was lying on her bed resting when she felt something land on her chest — it was a tarantula! She held her nerve and waited for it to crawl away. What she hated most of all were cockroaches; she found them 'loathsome'.

Driver ants ('bafumba') formed long colonies, which they aggressively defended against anything they encountered. The

Congo African grey parrot

larger, stronger ants flanked the smaller ants, while the fighter ants automatically took up positions as sentries, and set a perimeter corridor in which the smaller ants ran safely. Using their powerful cutting jaws, they attacked everything in their path, including snakes, birds and mammals. With their destructive bites and huge numbers, sometimes in excess of twenty-two million in a colony, as well as their habit of swarming into any opening in the body of their prey, such as the mouth and nose, they killed much larger animals than any other ant species.

Every night, they set out from their nests and went foraging. Occasionally Audrey was woken up by the sound of food scraps dropping from the thatched roof above her head, and she realized that her mud hut had been invaded. It was a hopeless task to try and fight them off; the only option was to escape until the ants had gone. Sometimes they ate chicks and destroyed the stores of the mission. When their foraging was over, they gathered themselves into columns with their food and were marshalled away, military style, by the fighter ants. The fierce rivalry among the villages meant that if an 'enemy prisoner' was caught, he was tied to a tree near a 'bafumba' nest and left to be eaten alive.

After heavy rain, when Audrey journeyed into the out-districts (villages within a 150-mile radius of the mission post), the water level was so high that much of the forest was submerged. The schoolboys offered to paddle her canoe straight through the submerged forested areas, thereby cutting off many of the twists and turns of the river, but these areas were infested with ants, mosquitoes and snakes, much to Audrey's dismay.

Trying to grow ordinary flowers such as roses was impossible. Bougainvillea and zinnias grew well, but they did not survive once cut and brought indoors. With no autumn in Congo, individual trees (and there were numerous species) lost their leaves at different times.

A typical day for Audrey

The day began for Audrey at 5:00 a.m. with personal devotions, which were interrupted by the sound of the 'talking drums'. Audrey's region of the Congo Basin was low-lying

A typical Congo scene

and fairly flat, except for the anthills that could reach ten to twenty feet in height. Each village selected their best anthill for a drum base. These traditional drums ('lokole') were cylindrical in shape, heavy and made from hollowed out tree trunks. Several of them were placed on top of the same anthill and were beaten to send messages. For instance, when it was time for church, the drums would sound to gather everyone together. So at 5:30 a.m. Audrey and the other missionaries heard the drums telling the villagers to get ready for morning prayers. At Baringa, a large mission station with a hospital, some 250 people — schoolboys, workmen and women from the nearby villages — crowded into the church, a building made out of mud with low walls and a thatched roof. Daily readings, similar to Scripture Union notes, called 'boloi' had been printed, so the teacher could follow a similar pattern each morning. On Sundays, when the pastor was preaching, the service usually lasted two hours.

By 6:30 a.m. it was light and the hospital work started. The sick travelled from miles around for treatment in the fairly well equipped hospital, and some of the Congolese workers were trained in medicine. For an hour before school, the boys cut the grass, weeded and generally tidied up, and every Friday they received pocket money ('poso'). Two of the priorities were to teach the women to read and to put the language down in writing. The former was a particular challenge because most of the women were involved in backbreaking work in the fields for most of the day and could not spare the time to learn. The latter was aided by a printing press at Bongandanga, which was the first in Congo.

At midday the drums sounded again to indicate the end of the morning's work, when Audrey returned to her house, where many children gathered in the hope of receiving 'a present' of some kind. Rest time was from 12:30 p.m. to 1:45 p.m., when the drums sounded the 'back to work' message. The workday ended at about 4:00 p.m., and between 4:00 p.m. and 5:30 p.m. each day there were various meetings including the 'baasi', an evening meeting to help those wanting to understand how to become a follower of the Lord Jesus Christ. By 6:00 p.m. it was dark and the Congolese returned to their villages.

Having eaten little all day, Audrey, along with the other missionaries, sat down and enjoyed their main meal together. At around 7:00 p.m. they heard singing and dancing to the sound of drums coming from the villages. At full moon these musical celebrations went on all night! Finally, at about 11:00 p.m., after the preparations for the next day had been finished, it was time for bed. As Audrey climbed under her mosquito net, she shone her flashlight at her feet, searching for jiggers — tiny flea-like creatures that bore into toes. The female jiggers produced their eggs in small sacs under the skin, causing irritation to the victim, who then had to push a safety pin into the toe to dig out the sac of eggs without breaking it. Only after this nightly ritual was over could Audrey lie down to sleep in peace.

10
Tying the knot

Learning the language

Dr and Mrs Wright, Mr and Mrs Campbell (and their respective children) and two single missionaries staffed the Baringa mission station, where Audrey stayed for three or four months to learn the tonal Lomongo language of the Congolese. Great emphasis was placed on learning the language well — the secret of working with another people group — and Audrey spent a great deal of time just listening to how the Africans spoke. On account of Congo being a Belgian Colony, no English was spoken. French was the language of the government, but the natives spoke only tribal languages.

In the afternoons, Audrey, accompanying Ella Campbell, visited women, who had been busy for hours in the manioc fields. They smiled at her and greeted her in a friendly way. She listened intently to their conversations, enjoyed their sense of humour, and was sometimes taken into a women's class and up to the hospital, where she was encouraged not to be shy, but to use the language as much as possible. Eventually she spoke more freely with them. She was not yet in a position to teach them, but she encouraged them to read 'beginners books', which had been printed on the presses at Bongandanga.

At Redcliffe she had been given good general instruction about missionary life, but there was no one at the college able to teach the different Congolese languages. Redcliffe's main emphasis had been to teach Jesus Christ, a rock on whom all missionaries can depend, proving him to be sufficient in every situation, and on being absolutely sure of a calling to missionary service, which entailed a life-long commitment. To live among the Congolese was, in Audrey's view, the only way to learn the language adequately.

As well as the language itself Audrey had to learn the customs behind the language. For instance, the Congolese greeting '*oetso*', equivalent to our 'good morning', meant 'you have come alive'. The tribes were so bound up in the realm of spirits that they did not build any windows in their houses because they believed that when asleep, their spirits came out of their bodies, climbed out the windows and went 'walkabout'. They used to ask the missionaries, who slept in houses with windows, 'Where will the spirits go and how will they know when and where to return?' So their morning greeting '*oetso*' was an acknowledgement that your spirit had returned and you were alive! The correct response was: 'You have also come alive?' If the missionaries saw them later on in the day, they said, 'Oh, you're still there?' and they replied, 'You are there?' All day long the natives sat outside their mud houses, but around 9:00 p.m. they went inside and shut the door so their spirits could not escape.

After three or four months of language study at Baringa, Audrey was examined to determine her progress; the exam included giving a simple talk in the Lomongo language. Thankfully she passed.

The mission station

The pioneer missionaries to Congo initially faced tremendous hostility from the natives. Their first main objective was to win over the tribal chief and to get his permission to live within the community. They then needed land on which to build, sometimes a forested area that had to be cleared and made ready for the mission station. When finished, the station usually comprised missionaries' homes, a church and school, small houses for the nurses and others in training, a carpentry shop to make desks and tables, cook houses, toilet areas, and a hospital or just a dispensary and maternity ward. A couple with children were allowed their own house, while everyone else had to share.

Originally the hospital at Baringa was a mud building, but then the missionaries learned how to make sun dried bricks using a mould and kiln. The more modern structure had a central building for outpatients, with three or four wards. Each ward had about thirty wooden framed beds, which had been made at the mission station, and twine was used to support the patients' own sleeping mats. Many of the sick brought their whole family with them, who slept either in or under the patient's bed! There was also an operating theatre. The mission station was the centre of the community, a sort of parish with a radius of fifty to seventy miles.

Teaching children

The great desire of the early missionaries was to teach boys to read, so they established a school, and as some children travelled up to seventy miles to attend classes, dormitories were built to accommodate them. At the beginning of Audrey's time, the mission majored on primary education, even though children up to eighteen years of age attended. Secondary education followed some years later. The whole aim of the school was to lead boys to salvation, and by the time many of them left, they had become followers of the Lord Jesus Christ and wanted to become 'village teachers'. Village teachers were paid by the church and responsible for giving other boys and girls in their villages the rudiments of education, for helping them to understand Christian fundamentals and the Bible, and for showing them how to live hygienically.

A Roman Catholic mission known as the 'Mompes' was situated about twenty-five miles from Baringa, and children were allowed to choose whether to attend the Mompes or the Protestant mission school. As far as the state was concerned, they preferred to take boys from the Protestant mission school because they were 'more honest', although there were exceptions. Audrey recalled that a colleague knew that her houseboy was stealing sugar, so she tactfully told him, 'You must never take other people's goods', advice the boy ignored. One day she actually saw him stealing the sugar, so she challenged

Elleea

This photograph was actually taken on the Featherstones' way to Mompono and Yoseki after the Simba uprising (see chapters sixteen and seventeen). Elleea is talking with a Mongo mother and child.

him about it. He denied it. 'But I actually saw you!' retorted Audrey's colleague.

'Well, why didn't you say so!' replied the boy, as if to say that his crime was not so much stealing, but being found out.

Getting married

The time now arrived for Audrey to leave Baringa and to travel to Mompono to marry Elleea, whom she had not seen for eighteen months, apart from three or four days in Mompono. Margaret Brown, the single lady with whom she had been sharing a mission house, travelled by boat with her. Arthur Wright was to give her away, but at the time he was too busy to travel immediately, so he planned to join her later. The journey took three days and the two excited ladies were able to share a small cabin on the courier boat. The senior missionary couple, Mr and Mrs Hanson, met them at Mompono and Mr Hanson, the principal of the training school at Mompono, was to conduct the ceremony. There were two other single ladies, but no one else.

As Audrey stepped off the boat, she felt apprehensive about getting married and afraid of the future. What should she do? To whom could she turn? She did not know what to do. She was only twenty-four and surrounded by people who were strangers to her. She wanted to share her fears and doubts, and to seek the wisdom of a trusted friend, but, humanly speaking, there was no one in whom she could confide.

She had never dreamed of a big wedding because she had never wanted to get married! So when she discovered there were no presents, no cake, no confetti and none of the other things associated with a lavish English wedding she was not unduly worried. However, she was pleased that Mabel Hanson had been given the job of organizing a meal after the ceremony.

The day before the wedding, there was no sign of Arthur Wright, and Audrey started to panic. Then at about 11:00 p.m. she heard the sound of a motorbike — suddenly Arthur Wright and Gilbert Campbell appeared covered in mud and absolutely exhausted after riding hundreds of miles over very

Audrey and Elleea's wedding day, 12 June 1947.

Back row left to right: Mrs Blohm (Belgian administrator's wife), Mr Blohm (Belgian administrator), Gilbert Campbell, Len Hanson, Arthur Wright, Mr and Mrs Walling.
Front row left to right: Mabel Hanson, Elleea, Audrey, Valerie Walling, Vera Haas.

rough terrain. The local Belgian administrator and his wife also travelled many miles in order to be present.

So the big day dawned, 12 June 1947. Audrey still felt trapped. The drums started to beat and many Congolese, who had heard that Elleea (the Congolese called him 'Botuli', a prestigious African name meaning 'blacksmith') was getting married, arrived from far and near. 'He is getting his own "Mama",' they declared, although they did not understand why he was taking such a step after thirteen years in Congo, for their concept of marriage was completely different to ours in the West. They were polygamists and marriages were arranged. A man paid a dowry of goats, or money (the Belgian franc), or gold — anything of value — to the family of the girl he was to marry and as soon as that was paid the couple were considered married.

Audrey wore a simple white dress with a veil she had made out of parachute silk, around which she had sewn some beautiful Belgian lace that she had bought in Antwerp. Her bouquet was a tiny spray of local flowers. The church was packed and outside there was a vast sea of 'black faces' watching every move. Arthur escorted Audrey to the front of the church, where Gilbert the best man was waiting. Len Hanson, a large man, was standing ready to officiate and of course Elleea was there. It was a traditional service but conducted in three different languages: French for the benefit of the Belgian couple, English and Lomongo. Each part was said three times by Len Hanson. When he spoke the words, 'Until death do us part,' the congregation, with hands over their mouths, gasped in shock, that the 'white missionaries' were promising to remain faithful to each other for life, a commitment unheard of as far as they were concerned.

After the ceremony they had a quick drink of orange juice before jumping in a truck, along with Arthur, and riding to the nearest state post some fifteen miles away to be 'properly married' by a Belgian lawyer, a Mr Finaulst. They received a marriage book, not a certificate, and then at sunset they returned to Mompono, where, with a few friends, they enjoyed a reception meal.

Mr and Mrs Young, an elderly missionary couple nearing retirement, had written to Elleea inviting him and his new wife to spend their honeymoon at Bongandanga. Two days after the wedding, the happy couple made the long and difficult journey to Bongandanga. At the end of their weeklong stay, Len Hanson arrived to take them home. Mr Young said 'good-bye' and handed them an envelope. Inside was a note: 'The first year is the worst!' — that is all it said. With that rather pessimistic warning in their hearts, they returned to Mompono.

In spite of Audrey's earlier fears, she felt secure with Elleea. He was just right for her — strong where she was weak, courageous when she was afraid, an experienced missionary, who was able to guide her through the ups and downs of life in Congo. They enjoyed many happy years together.

11
A steep learning curve

Elleea was working hard at Mompono, where he was responsible for seeing that everything at the mission station was running properly. He helped the pastors with their work in the churches, taught in seekers' meetings, and visited the surrounding villages, where he preached and instructed young believers in the fundamental doctrines of the Christian faith.

Assessed

During the first three years in Congo, Audrey, while adjusting to a completely different lifestyle and to the new customs and language, was assessed in all that she did and continually came under 'RBMU's spotlight'. One of the pressures she felt keenly was the fact that if a new missionary did not grasp the language within the first term of service (essentially a trial period), she could be sent home as unsuitable for the field. She also experienced difficulties in the fact that she was married to a senior missionary, which meant she needed to 'keep her ears open and her mouth shut', not always an easy discipline for her to follow.

Senior missionaries made it their business to ensure that she was progressing not only in language study, but in integration — that she mixed well and that her manner towards the Congolese was kind, gracious and demonstrated a genuine affection for the people and a deep and sincere love for the Lord Jesus Christ. An arrogant or unkind attitude was regarded as a serious offence and reprehensible. At the end of her first three years, the senior missionaries wrote a report on her that went to

Mompono Bible School

the field superintendent and council. At the annual field conference, after Audrey had been asked to leave the meeting room, the report was read out, an experience that Audrey found both 'intimidating and humbling'. A copy of the report was given to her, which detailed her good and not so good points.

Audrey was in the unusual position of being a new young missionary married to an experienced senior missionary, who was expected to move to any area where there was a staffing need for church and pastoral workers. After she had been married for only three or four months, a need at Lulonga, where a single lady was in sole charge, was made known. This was brought to the field conference and the lot fell on Elleea and Audrey to go. Audrey found this particularly difficult, as the Lomongo language she had been trying so hard to learn was not spoken there. She was also due to take a big language exam at the end of the year. However, she had no choice but to follow her husband and they worked together in Lulonga for a year.

At the end of the year they asked the field conference if they could remain as they were settled and had built up a healthy relationship with the people. At first this arrangement was agreed upon, but on the last day of the conference, the leaders asked to speak with Elleea, who later passed on the news to Audrey: 'We have to work at Ikau — 250 miles away!' Audrey was devastated. Her only consolation was that at Ikau they spoke Lomongo. At the time no reason for the unexpected move was given to Audrey, but later she found out that there had been a crisis at Ikau between staff members, who needed to be replaced.

So in her first three years, Audrey had worked in Mompono, Lulonga and Ikau, an unusual and trying time for her, which accentuated her sense of insecurity and diffidence, and, with an 'uncertain upbringing and background' still bothering her, made her ask the question, 'Where do I belong?' It is therefore not surprising that her 'end of first term report' stated that she had not shown enough initiative in the work. However, the report, written in a gracious manner and which contained encouraging and helpful comments, did acknowledge that her first three-year term had been difficult, especially in the area of language study.

On furlough

The Featherstones started for home on their first furlough early in 1950.They travelled by ship via Antwerp, a journey which took approximately three weeks. During the last three years neither of them had had a day off so the journey home was a wonderful opportunity to relax and unwind.

After a couple of weeks' rest in England, they were presented with their programme of deputation events for the next ten months, which involved almost continual travel all over Great Britain. RBMU was dependent on the financial and prayer support of Christians in different parts of the country and that support was only kept 'alive' by the hard work of missionaries on furlough.

Sometimes Audrey and Elleea travelled together, sometimes alone, carrying their heavy photographic slides. Churches that had supported missionaries for years were keen for them to speak either at a single meeting or at big missionary weekends. The Saturday evening meetings were usually packed with young and old and on Sundays they were asked to share their 'missionary experiences'. Audrey was not a natural 'up front person' and she felt inadequate for the task, but once she started talking about Congo her inhibitions soon left her.

In their travels they stayed in a number of different homes, some of which reminded Audrey of Congo! Once she had to go to Stoke-on-Trent for a weekend, and on arrival at Stoke railway station a small man, holding in full view an RBMU magazine for identification, met her. 'Follow me,' he said. After a long bus journey to the outskirts of Stoke, she was dropped at a modest terraced house, where a man and his wife lived with their young son. His wife seemed a bit overwhelmed at having Audrey stay and nervously showed 'the great missionary' to her bedroom, which was obviously the son's room. There was no bathroom in the house, just a bowl of water, and the toilet was 'in the yard'. As she pulled back the bedcovers to climb into bed, it was apparent by the stains on the sheets that the bed had not been changed for some considerable time!

Sometimes Audrey and Elleea stayed at RBMU Mission headquarters at Upper Norwood; at other times they visited friends around the country. The constant travelling was not only tiring, but it also made it difficult for them to prepare properly ahead of meetings. During this furlough, Audrey renewed contact with her mother, who had moved to Brixham with her new husband. On hearing that she had become a Christian, her mother simply put it down to a 'funny phase her daughter was passing through', but she thought her life as a missionary was a 'good work' and 'very commendable'.

After nearly a year on furlough, both Audrey and Elleea were longing to return to Congo.

12
A second term

Lulonga

The Featherstones' second term in Congo was from 1951 to early 1955. They arrived in time for the October conference, when staffing issues were again raised. They were asked to return to Lulonga because only one missionary was stationed there. Lulonga, situated on the banks of the Lulonga and Congo rivers, was an area of thick forest with a multitude of tributaries and streams. There were no roads and the only means of transport was by canoe.

The Lingombe tribe spoke Lingombe, a different language to Lomongo, but with the same construction of grammar. The Mongo and Lingombe tribes had a history of bitter rivalry and it was a great achievement of the ruling Belgians to prevent them from massacring each other.

The spirit world

The tribes were receptive to spiritual teaching, although they were very superstitious. Charms were worn from an early age to ward off evil spirits. When someone died and was buried, the ground in front of the grave was levelled, and their spear, bowl, leopard skin mat and other personal possessions were placed there ready to be taken to the 'new world', where spirit and body were reunited.

Once a man from a nearby village had gone across the river and been killed by a crocodile. When he did not come home, his wife and others were worried and went to look for him.

Eventually they found part of his dismembered body at the side of the river in the forest. Amidst loud wailing, with people throwing themselves around in anguish, they managed to bring back parts of the body for burial. They made a huge hole in the side of an anthill and put the body inside, covering it over. They also made a ledge on which they put all his belongings. When Audrey asked why they did this, they replied, 'Because we don't know where he is going; he will need his possessions in the life to which he has gone.' Then they cut themselves to show their grief.

They believed the person's spirit would enter a tree or a crocodile, return to the village, and take revenge on anyone who had done him harm. If they saw a rogue elephant, they were convinced that a dead man's spirit had entered that animal. The missionaries keenly sensed the spirit world and the fear in which the Africans lived.

The witch doctor was a powerful member of the community and greatly revered. When the sick went to him, he accused them of antagonizing one of the spirits. Occasionally he placed a curse on someone and they died. If a man was accused of stealing, he was dragged to the witch doctor, who made up various potions. If, according to their beliefs, the accused drank the potions and survived, he was not guilty; if he died, he had received just recompense for his crime. Audrey and Elleea had no clash personally with the witch doctor, but their teaching that Jesus Christ could free men and women from the clutches of Satan obviously contradicted his ideas and made him hostile to them.

Generally the villagers were happy and enjoyed dancing at night. Men danced together, re-enacting a story from their ancestors, and children and women danced together. In time, the people grew to like the missionaries, especially when they realized they were there to help them. The medical work was a tremendous influence for good. The villagers first took their sick to the witch doctor, but when their condition worsened, they travelled, sometimes for miles, to the mission hospital.

Crossing the Congo River (September 1954)

Visiting the out-districts

By this time Audrey was proficient enough in the tribal language to teach the women and children, and she accompanied Elleea on his visits to the out-districts. On these visits, as they climbed out of the canoe, the drums started to sound and many of the tribes' people came to welcome them, which caused quite a commotion. Some were already Christians, having been led to Christ by the Congolese pastor or catechist teacher; others were still heathen. A small mud hut was vacated for the visitors, who laid out their camp beds and mosquito nets, leaving little room in which to move. They stayed about a week and took time to speak and pray with the pastor and elders and to hold teaching meetings, to which about fifty villagers came.

They put on 'lantern shows' for the tribes' people, courtesy of a hurricane lamp, projecting slides onto a piece of white material, which served as a screen. The Congolese watched the pictures of animals, trees and people with rapt attention. The pastors, elders and teachers, who owned their own Bibles, then preached in a vivid and dramatic fashion, making stories such as Elijah on Mount Carmel with the priests of Baal come alive before the congregation. The preachers applied the Scriptures in a way the people could identify with and understand.

During one of Audrey and Elleea's visits to the out-districts, as they were getting ready for bed with a hurricane lamp burning, they heard scratching noises coming from outside. When they investigated they discovered a group of children at the side of the hut, boring holes with their fingers through the mud walls, through which they could watch what the white missionaries were doing! They chased them away so they could undress in private. Back at the mission station, Audrey and Elleea had a veranda outside their bedroom and occasionally after they had retired to bed, they were conscious of children watching them through the windows — curiosity had got the better of them. The couple were 'not amused!'

After a week in the same place they moved on to the next cluster of villages, where they were again received warmly and often presented with eggs. They accepted them by putting their open hands together as a gesture of gratitude. Sometimes on their way home they heard cheeping coming from the basket and they knew the eggs had hatched! The villagers never ate the eggs themselves, but carefully took them from the mother hen and presented them to the missionaries.

After Elleea had concluded his studies at All Nations Missionary Training College, he had attended Livingstone College in Bow, which specialized in medical work. There he had learned how to deliver babies, extract teeth, dress wounds and all the basics of how to help sick people on the mission field. All the tribes' people had intestinal worms, which they believed helped them to function properly, but in reality they caused all sorts of health problems, and Elleea often had to deal with a long queue of people wanting his medical help. Audrey did her best to assist.

After visiting the villages in the out-districts for about four or five weeks, they returned to the mission station, where they stayed for a similar length of time.

It was during their time in Lulonga that Elleea suffered a bad accident. Along with a couple of Congolese workmen, he was trying to replace a large wooden beam in the roof of a house. As they were positioning it, one of the workmen lost his grip. The beam fell and landed on Elleea's head, causing a horrible gash, which bled profusely. He was stitched up, but the wound became infected. It eventually healed, but Elleea was badly shaken by the whole episode.

Altogether they spent a year in Lulonga before moving to Yuli in 1952 for the next six years.

Yuli

Yuli was very much in the wilds, with dirt tracks for roads, and lying in the midst of a network of streams, rivers and tributaries, which were not big enough to take the courier boats; so Audrey and Elleea had to paddle through the mango swamps and creeks in canoes. In the 1940/50s the colonial government made a road from Bosodjafo, west of Yuli, down to Boende and back to Mbandaka. When the work started the state enlisted the help of villagers, who were responsible for the particular section of the road nearest to their village. Although the road

Elleea and Audrey at Yuli (1952)

made the villages more accessible, the track from Yuli to the main road was often flooded and impassable, and Audrey and Elleea were at times 'cut off' from the surrounding area.

During these six years, the missionaries, Congolese pastors and village teachers were telling everyone they could about the true God, the Lord Jesus Christ, and the way of salvation — all against the backdrop of heathen beliefs and spiritism. The Congolese put up fetishes everywhere to ward off evil spirits, and any bad experience such as disease or death was attributed to a 'bad' spirit.

Teaching

For the missionaries, their starting point in preaching Christ was the word 'God', for the villagers believed in a Supreme Being, Nzakomba, who had created all things and was 'in charge' of the world, but they did not know him personally. They regarded him as an all-powerful, omnipresent, 'great' spirit, with emotions like themselves. He could get angry or be good to them, if they placated him.

In the Lomongo language there is no word for love. The nearest words that express true love, and that God is a God who loves, are the words translated 'longing pain', a pain that strongly desires something, for instance, a mother in her 'longing and concern' for her children. This was the most appropriate way in which Audrey was able to convey the idea of love. She also had difficulty in trying to explain to them the Triune God, and in translating phrases like 'God is our Rock', for the Congolese only knew about deep forest — there were no rocks to point out to them, so she had to start with something they could understand. She had to teach them a strange new concept: that there is one God who reveals himself in his Son. These language difficulties made her determined to help them read the Bible for themselves.

When she sat down with them to explain the Bible, she always prayed for the Holy Spirit to enlighten them. Their understanding of the Old Testament was good; the days of the patriarchs were akin to their mindset, and they were fascinated by such stories as Moses and the burning bush. They understood

Sixth anniversary of 'Christian Endeavour' boys' Bible study group (1954)

that God's spirit was a good 'sacred' spirit. Audrey used the word Yahweh for God's name and 'Fear Yahweh' was a text on the wall in one of the small churches. In all that she said she tried to convey the true character of the living creator God and then to explain the life and work of Jesus. She talked about sin and how God hated anything that was evil, which they understood from their own beliefs. They used strong words to describe evil and saw sin in terms of the cruel things that others did to them. As their fear of spirits was so real, Audrey often repeated the message that the Son of God came from heaven to earth to deliver people from fear.

The women were not sceptical or suspicious of Audrey's teachings; they were eager to understand and were accepting of what was said. Many came to believe in Jesus and Audrey was overjoyed to see the change that took place in their lives, and to see them attending women's meetings, where Congolese women who had been led to the Lord addressed the congregations with vibrancy and displayed a good grasp of God's love and what it was to possess eternal life.

Journey back to Congo

Early in 1955, the Featherstones returned home for their overdue year-long furlough, after which they asked RBMU if they could return to Congo by boat on the Union Castle line via Suez and East Africa, a journey that would at least give them a few weeks break. RBMU agreed to this request.

At the beginning of 1956, Audrey and Elleea boarded the Warwick Castle (Union Castle line) at Tilbury and enjoyed relaxing on an English boat where everyone spoke their language. They made friends with a missionary couple working in Uganda with Africa Inland Mission (AIM) and spent many hours enjoying their company. The ship sailed across the Mediterranean to Egypt, through the Suez Canal, down the Red Sea to Aden, where a BMS (Baptist Mission Society) missionary called Winifred Brown boarded. When the Warwick Castle docked at a Kenyan port, their AIM friends disembarked. Audrey and Elleea sailed on to Dar es Salaam, where Audrey never forgot walking through the town and hearing wonderful

The Featherstones' Land Rover in a ditch.
'Trying to extricate ourselves!'

Audrey at Tshuapa River crossing (1955)

African singing coming from the Anglican cathedral. From Dar es Salaam they boarded a train that took at least two days to reach the Tanganyika (now Tanzania) lakes, which were the end of the line.

It was the dry season and Audrey remembered the animals and the parched land — so different from Congo. During the journey they were able to visit Ujiji where Stanley met Livingstone in 1871 and uttered those now famous words, 'Dr Livingstone, I presume?' On the east side of Lake Tanganyika they had to wait for a boat to cross over to Congo, before another two days of travel by train north to Stanleyville. After four and a half years without a break and a hectic furlough, those weeks travelling back to Congo were a real joy and helped to prepare them for the upheavals of their third term.

Henry Morton Stanley

A statue of Henry Morton Stanley at Stanley Pool

Stanley meeting Livingstone:
'Dr Livingstone, I presume?'

Plaque where Stanley met Livingstone

13
Congo independence

The Featherstones returned to Congo with a new lease of life. Audrey spent time in the school, while Elleea travelled in the district evangelizing and preaching.

RBMU wanted to establish a sub mission post at Mpenzele, some fifteen to twenty miles south of Yuli, which was agreed to at the annual conference in 1958. With the conference's backing the Featherstones set about cutting down the forestation and starting a school in that area. They also erected a small house for themselves so they could live within walking distance of their latest project.

Countdown to independence

At this point Audrey and Elleea had no idea that Congo was heading towards independence, as 'in the bush' they were isolated from national politics. They were oblivious to the fact that two years earlier municipal elections had been held in Leopoldville and won by Abako, a political party championing the cause of the Bakongo tribal group and headed by Joseph Kasavubu, a staunch believer in a federalist independent Congo. Another more hot-headed politician emerging at the same time was Patrice Lumumba, a member of a minor tribe, who wanted the nation's future to be strongly centralized. In 1958 he founded Congo's first nationwide party, the Mouvement National Congolais.

While it is true to say that Belgium had done much to develop Congo's infrastructure, it had nevertheless failed to prepare adequately for the inevitability of independence and for a

Missionary conferences were annual events and often involved long journeys. During this tea break Audrey is leaning on the open front door of the Land Rover.

smooth transition of government to national rule. Many of its laws repressed the Congolese; under the 1908 Colonial Charter they were excluded from democratic participation in their own government and prevented, by a white European elite, from holding all but the lowest civil posts. A simmering resentment was first publicly expressed in 1956 in a Catholic school's periodical, which was followed by the Alliance of Bakongo, demanding a full bill of rights. Belgium's response was to offer a thirty-year timetable for emancipation.

When in 1958 France offered full independence to her African colonies, Patrice Lumumba petitioned the Belgian colonial minister to 'prepare the masses and the elite to take control of public affairs and free Congo from Colonialism'. He was supported by the majority of Congolese in the big towns, who demanded independence and wanted the Belgians to leave — 'Congo is our country and the wealth, commerce and banks belong to us, while every young black person has the right to a basic education' (eighty per cent of children enrolled in schools were restricted to a primary school education and there was only one university in Leopoldville).

Talks were soon undertaken in Brussels to consider the introduction of some greater measure of local autonomy, but riots broke out in Leopoldville in January 1959, and a wave of anti-white feeling swept the country. A scheduled political rally was banned, shops were looted, houses burned to the ground, Europeans attacked, and in response the police killed and wounded several Congolese. Belgium's king, Baudouin, in an effort to defuse the situation, declared his intention to give Congo full independence, and it was decided that elections for a territorial assembly would be held in December.

The announcement of elections launched intense political activity, but it was mainly along tribal lines, since almost no other allegiances had been formed. By November 1959 more than fifty political parties were officially registered, but only Lumumba's MNC had an essentially national perspective. At least two of the tribal parties represented such large regional groups that there was a strong possibility of secession. One was Joseph Kasavubu's ABAKO party and the other was the party

Audrey with a pineapple at the *lifeta*, Baringa (1960)

led by Moise Tshombe, based in the mineral-rich province of Katanga.

By the end of 1959, the Featherstones sensed the growing tension, which was occasionally confirmed by a Congolese Christian pastor or elder, who said reassuringly, 'If you hear rumours that we are going to take charge of everything, get rid of all that is colonial, and settle old scores, don't worry because you have been good people to us.'

Violence and elections

With mounting violence in the colony, and with the December elections invalid because of widespread boycotts, the Belgian government invited ninety-six delegates from the main Congolese parties to a conference in Brussels in January 1960. Lumumba, Kasavubu and Tshombe were among those who attended. The Belgians suggested a four-year transition to independence, but the Congolese refused to wait that long. By the end of the conference Belgium had agreed to the impractical step of Belgian Congo becoming an independent nation in less than six months. Part of the agreement stressed that over a period of two to three years Belgian experts would remain in the country to train Congolese to run the different administrations such as banks and government departments.

Meanwhile Audrey and Elleea were due for furlough in February/March 1960, but with Congo's independence looming in June, their field leader, Mike Wide, asked them to postpone it, so that missionary personnel would be on hand to man all the stations during the transition of power. Mike Wide reasoned that if there were no missionaries at a station, the Congolese would run riot there. So the Featherstones postponed their furlough until July.

In May the elections took place. Lumumba's MNC emerged as the largest single party, with Kasavubu's ABAKO the runners up. Neither party succeeded independently in forming a coalition, so as a compromise Kasavubu became president and head of state, and expressed goodwill towards Belgium; while Lumumba, an opponent of colonialism, became prime minister and the head of a coalition, which included twelve extremely diverse minor parties. Tshombe's party won control of the provincial assembly in Katanga.

Such an arrangement was a recipe for disaster, and only four days after independence (30 June 1960), when all seemed peaceful, with people rejoicing and dancing in the villages, there was mutiny among the soldiers. The reason behind the trouble was that, in spite of independence, the officers in the Congolese army were without exception white — hardly a surprising fact, as in the colonial army Africans could not rise higher than the rank of sergeant major, and in the rush to independence the first Congolese officer cadets had not yet completed their courses!

In order to quell the rising tension Lumumba, during the first week of July, agreed to dismiss all the Belgian officers and to appoint Congolese in their places. Joseph Mobutu, the minister for defence, issued the new commissions. In reality no one was able to control the unfolding chaos and, without any effective chain of command, the army went on the rampage, attacking the Belgian population. Priests in particular were violently abused and nuns raped. Before the middle of July 25,000 Belgians had fled the country, while 10,000 Belgian paratroopers had been flown into Congo to protect European lives and property, particularly in Katanga.

On 11 July, Moise Tshombe, taking advantage of the collapse of government control, declared the independence of Katanga, the nation's richest province, and at the same time asked for Belgian military aid. With the help of Belgian troops he expelled all units of the Congolese army. The Lumumba government appealed to the U.N. for military assistance in an attempt to suppress the army mutiny.

A dangerous journey

In the midst of this violent disruption and uncertainty, RBMU's executive committee decided to hold their field conference in July rather than October so that the mission could evaluate the situation and decide what to do next. They sent a message to the Featherstones, 'Please travel to Ikau as quickly as possible.' They were the only missionaries at Mpenzele — the

The Featherstones' home in Mpenzele for a few months prior to Congo independence

other two workers had remained at Yuli — and consequently felt extremely vulnerable. At the time Audrey was alone in the forest as Elleea had gone to collect funds from Basankusu, but the message reached him somehow and he hurried back to Mpenzele.

They threw a few belongings into their Land Rover, not realizing they would never return to Mpenzele, yet fully aware by now that the whole of Congo was erupting into anarchy. They started the long journey towards Ikau. As they travelled, the villagers, rather than coming out to greet them, just stared at them in stony silence. Many cars and vehicles were travelling in the opposite direction — everyone who was white, Belgians and Portuguese, were escaping to Mbandaka. Sometimes they were stopped and asked where they were going. Many urged them to turn around because in the areas where white people had been living, there was mutiny, with looting and pillaging.

They drove on through unfamiliar territory, with people still glaring at them, but eventually they crossed the Ikelemba River. Then disaster struck. The Land Rover in which they were travelling broke down and they needed a push start to get it going again. Audrey was nervous as people from the nearby village gathered around. 'Are they going to help push us or are they going to kill us?' thought Audrey. After what seemed like an eternity, they agreed to push. By this time it was late afternoon and they still had a long way to go. The sun soon sank beneath the horizon, and as they passed through village after village, they heard the drums beating and people dancing wildly. Eventually, in the early hours of the next morning, they arrived at Ikau.

An important decision

Some thirty to forty missionaries gathered in Ikau. Although there was tension all around, Audrey was greatly encouraged to be with other believers and to pray with them. They were informed that a plane was soon to land and that all single ladies and those with young children were to leave, for it was too dangerous to stay.

The Congolese pastors and elders then asked the remaining group, 'Will you please pray about whether or not all of you should leave? Could some of you older couples stay?' They felt that the soldiers, many of whom had already mutinied, were just waiting for all the white people to leave; then they could take control of everything — the mission houses, hospitals, schools etc. If some missionaries stayed, the pastors thought it might provide stability and a restraining influence, although they recognized the risk involved. After they had discussed the various options, Lilian Ivimey led the group in devotions, speaking on the verse 'God is our refuge and strength.' It was a 'precious' and much needed time.

Audrey and Elleea knew it was the right decision to stay, along with seven others: Alfred and Lilian Ivimey, Sebo and Mali Baoitti, Raymond Brooks, and Mike and Isobel Wide. Later it was discovered that the soldiers had indeed invaded those mission stations that were left without staff. In addition, at some missions, where all the personnel had left for their own safety, when the missionaries tried to return, they were told by the Congolese, 'You ran away; now we don't want you.'

The nine of them said an emotional farewell to their fellow missionaries, not knowing what would become of them. After their colleagues had departed all seemed 'very odd' to Audrey as she listened to the distant humming of outboard motors from the river taking white people down to Mbandaka in order to flee the country.

For those who remained the outlook was bleak. Many Congolese had imbibed the nationalist spirit and regarded independence as more than 'merely throwing off the yoke of colonial rule'. For them it was a reversal of roles: 'Now Congolese are in charge. Foreigners must take orders.' Even many church leaders 'hotly demanded complete relinquishment of all missionary control — funds, properties, and institutional administration. Church-mission tensions developed. Fellowship was strained.'

Many politicians in the West demonstrated support for Tshombe at this time, no doubt mindful of the wealth of his region, while Lumumba asked the Soviets for help in recovering Katanga. During August, Russian aircraft, arms, technicians and military advisors arrived, making the independence of Congo a potential flashpoint of the Cold War. These explosive issues dominated debate in the general assembly of the U.N., whose forces on the ground tried to maintain peace. In the event, a local coup proved a turning point.

14
Furlough at last!

The Featherstones stayed at Ikau for three to four weeks, just waiting to see what was going to happen next, and yet noticing that even the young men out in the bush were affected by the anarchy sweeping through the country. Eventually they travelled to Baringa, along with Mike and Isobel Wide. They were well received and settled down, ready to return home and enjoy their furlough that was nearly six months overdue.

On 4 September, President Kasavubu announced that he had dismissed Lumumba as prime minister. Lumumba, in a desperate act to save his own position, hurried to a radio station to broadcast that he had dismissed Kasavubu as president. The resulting confusion was only resolved when the minister of defence, Mobutu Sese Seko, declared ten days later that he was 'neutralizing' all politicians and was temporarily taking over the duties of government in the name of the army.

The journey home

While the political leaders battled it out for supremacy, Audrey and Elleea drove to Basankusu, near Ikau, where there was an airfield and they boarded a small plane to Leopoldville. There were no other white people at Leopoldville airport, and as they looked around wondering what to do next, they only saw U.N. army transport planes of all different nationalities. Around the perimeter of the airfield were hundreds of suitcases belonging to the people who had fled the country a couple of months earlier. There were bullet holes everywhere. They walked towards the airport building, but there was no one there except

U.N. personnel, who wondered who they were and what they were doing. They asked if it was possible to get into the centre of town so they could stay at the guest house there, but the military men answered, 'No way!' They asked if there were any planes going to Europe, but again the answer was an emphatic, 'No way!'

The Sabena airline route was through South Africa and Rhodesia, but on account of Katanga's independence, planes heading back to Belgium flew up from South Africa to Elizabethville, where they took on passengers. They would not fly on to Leopoldville, for the central government feared passengers would be imprisoned. The U.N. personnel explained the situation to Audrey and Elleea, who by now were extremely hungry and thirsty, not having had anything to eat or drink since breakfast. Apparently it was just too dangerous to try and reach the guest house. The U.N. promised to take them over the river to French Congo, to Brazzaville, where there was an airport. 'Wait here while we search for someone to take you.' So they waited patiently.

One of the U.N. personnel returned and told them that arrangements had been made for them to cross into French Congo. They were taken to a huge transport plane with Arabic writing on the side and no seats. The pilot duly arrived and flew them to Brazzaville — a ten-minute flight over Stanley Pool. Apart from the pilot they were the only ones on board.

They arrived at about midnight but had no currency to buy food or drink. They were advised that a Sabena passenger plane was flying up from Elizabethville in the early hours, which they gratefully boarded at about 2:00 a.m. There were just two seats left and they were next to each other. Audrey remembered feeling 'so cold'. As they dozed she was aware of the plane landing. She peered out of the window and as the plane trundled along the runway to a stop, she was highly amused at where they had landed — Timbuktu! Up to that time she had no idea that such a place existed. No one disembarked so she assumed the plane was refuelling.

She dozed again, and when she awoke the plane was flying over the Sahara and the sun was just coming up. She could see the Mediterranean ahead. It was a beautiful sight. They continued over the toe of Italy and landed in Rome, where they disembarked for a two-hour stopover. A coach arrived and took them to a restaurant, where they satisfied their hunger and thirst, after which, on a gloriously sunny day, they re-boarded the plane. They flew up the northwest coast of Italy and over Switzerland, and as they were flying fairly low, Audrey could clearly see the mountains, valleys, lakes, and even the chalets. As they neared Brussels the sky became overcast and grey. They changed planes in Brussels and flew to London. When they arrived it was late afternoon and raining.

Audrey and Elleea were home for only about six months and engaged in a busy programme of deputation work. Congo was headline news at the time and so naturally everyone was particularly interested to hear about their work.

Filariasis

During their furlough, they spent some time with Audrey's mother and her new husband in Brixham, Devon, where they were now living. When Audrey showed her mother some swellings that had started to appear all over her body, she suggested an appointment with the local surgery; so off Audrey and Elleea went to see one of the doctors, who kindly asked, 'What can I do for you?' Audrey explained about the swellings. The doctor looked at them and then at Audrey. 'Have you always lived in this country?' he asked.

'No,' replied Audrey.

'Do you live and work in the tropics, in Africa?'

'Yes,' said Audrey, rather startled at the doctor's discerning questions.

'You have loa loa filariasis' (also called loiasis and African eyeworm), was the doctor's diagnosis, 'a skin and eye disease that is caused by the nematode worm, loa loa filaria. Humans contract this disease through the bite of a horsefly, or mango fly. It causes red itchy swellings below the skin called "Calabar swellings". It is possible,' continued the doctor, 'to be bitten without realizing it. When the flies bite they inject their eggs into the bloodstream. In due time the eggs hatch out into worms.

If the larvae get into a lymph gland, they block it and cause a condition similar to elephantiasis.'

Audrey knew about the disease, but was obviously surprised to have contracted it. The doctor asked, 'Where in Africa do you work?'

'Congo'.

To Audrey's amazement the doctor said that he had been working there too! His name was Ian Sharp and he and his wife, also named Audrey, were UFM (The Unevangelized Fields Mission) missionaries. Like thousands of others, they and their small children had fled the country just after independence.

He asked Audrey and Elleea, 'Are you going back?'

'Yes, we hope to quite soon. What are you going to do?'

He replied, 'I am praying hard about what to do. The need out there is so great, but I have a family for whom I am responsible, so we have to be very sure it is God's will for us to return.' Audrey and Elleea agreed and said they would pray for him that in due time he might know what to do. He prescribed the drug diethylcarbamazine (DEC), which has unpleasant side effects, and which they had to go to Torquay to collect. When Audrey took the drug she felt so ill she wanted to die; irritation was a particular problem. The drug killed the larvae, but she still experienced many re-occurrences of the disease after her return to Congo, and in later life she suffered from Onchocerciasis, or 'river blindness', the world's second leading infectious cause of blindness.

After seeing the doctor, Audrey visited an optician, who commented, 'There is something at the back of your eye that I don't understand — you need to go to Torbay Hospital.' There they diagnosed the damage to the eye caused by loa loa filariasis, which, to Audrey's dismay, could not be repaired.

Some time later the Featherstones heard shocking news. Dr and Mrs Ian Sharp, with their three children, had indeed returned to Congo, where in 1964 Simba rebels captured the whole family. They were taken down to the riverbank, cut into pieces and thrown into the water — massacred like so many other missionaries working near Stanleyville at that time.

15
Back to Congo

Unstable times

Back in Congo, deposed premier Lumumba unwisely left Leopoldville, where he had been living under U.N. protection. He was captured by troops loyal to Kasavubu and sent in January 1961 to Katanga. He was last seen on arrival in Katanga being transferred, blindfolded and handcuffed, from a plane to a waiting car. Mobutu had planned to try him for inciting the army to rebellion and other crimes, but on 17 January he was mysteriously murdered either by Katangan police or Belgian mercenaries. Evidence emerged years later to suggest that both President Eisenhower and the Belgian government were party to plans to eliminate this left-wing African leader.

Mobutu, secretly in Kasavubu's camp and with the encouragement of the C.I.A., who was alarmed at Lumumba's 'communist policy', closed down the Soviet embassy. In February he returned the government to Kasavubu and was duly appointed commander of the army.

During 1961 and 1962 the urgent question in Congo was whether Tshombe could sustain an independent Katanga. He had the support of the powerful mining company, Union Minière, and his army was strengthened by the continuing presence of Belgian troops and the addition of European mercenaries; but the U.N. and the majority of international opinion were against the secession of Katanga. Outbreaks of fighting and bursts of urgent U.N. diplomacy alternated during this period, with Tshombe reneging on promises whenever it suited him.

Congo bound

It was into this volatile and dangerous situation that the Featherstones returned in the early summer of 1961. They arrived at Heathrow on a grey, drizzly afternoon, with rumbles of thunder in the air and a gale blowing. Audrey wondered if they would be allowed to take off, but it was soon confirmed that they could leave for Brussels. On account of it being a fairly short trip, the plane flew low, but they still endured severe turbulence.

They landed in Brussels in the early evening ready for the night flight down to Leopoldville. They hurried around the airport for departure details and then heard on the loudspeaker that, because of the storm, which had grown even worse, they could not leave that night. Hotel accommodation was provided for them.

By the morning the storm had passed; they were told to assemble and wait for the bus to take them back to the airport. While waiting for the bus, they heard that the flight was further delayed because of mechanical trouble. They arrived at the airport at about 10:00 a.m. and saw the plane stationed on the tarmac. As they boarded, Audrey saw the mechanics still screwing something back together, which did not fill her with a great deal of confidence for the forthcoming flight! At midday they took off for Geneva, where they waited until the early evening for their flight to Leopoldville. Assured they were on the right plane, they settled back in their seats.

As they were flying southwards, Elleea suddenly nudged Audrey and said, 'Do you see what it says there?' There was a notice in front of them, which they had not seen before, which said Elizabethville (Lubumbashi). Now Elizabethville was right down in the southeast, almost into Zambia, and hundreds of miles from Leopoldville. They both panicked. They called to the stewardess, who explained that VIP passengers from the Katanga province were on board. Katanga had seceded from central government, which meant that if the plane had landed in Leopoldville, the VIPs would have been arrested and thrown in prison, so they had to drop them off at Elizabethville, which they did at about 2:00 a.m.

At Elizabethville everyone left the plane. Armed Katangan soldiers shepherded the passengers into a small room, while the VIPs were driven away. About an hour later they re-boarded the plane and flew back to Leopoldville in the middle of another severe thunder and lightning storm.

Back in Congo

Joseph Conley paints a gloomy picture of the chaos that greeted returning missionaries after independence. 'Hundreds of primary schools were in the hands of headmasters who had nothing more than elementary schooling. The sudden flush of power had unmasked an unsuspected spiritual adolescence within the national church leadership. Baptisms were conducted without adequate Biblical instruction. Principles instilled carefully over years were cavalierly discarded or waived in the expediency of the moment. Standards were lowered as patriotic fervour infused a revived respect for former tribal superstitions and the animism of yesteryear.' Thankfully there was a remnant that remained faithful to Christ and his teachings.

In September/October, Audrey and Elleea attended RBMU's field conference in Ikau. As so many missionaries had gone home after independence and RBMU's numbers were depleted, the conference discussed the question: 'How can eleven main mission stations be manned?' It was reluctantly agreed that it was not possible to staff some of the smaller stations, such as Yuli. The Featherstones were asked to go to Baringa.

CADELU

Back in 1902 the Congo Protestant Council (a cooperative affiliation of Protestant missions) had been established, and each mission organization had its own field and independence, with little friction between them. In 1956 the CPC changed from a council of mission agencies to a council of churches, with Congolese voting. With independence the CPC decided that its leadership would comprise of Congolese nationals only and that foreigners could remain only as technical aides. In order to deal effectively with the government, it was considered necessary for the missions to speak with one voice and to have someone to represent the Protestant churches, so they chose a secretary-general. His name was Pastor Pierre Shaumba. He testified, along with others, that as the gospel had spread, thousands of his people had professed faith in Christ, and were in need of further teaching to deepen their new beliefs.

By 1960, RBMU had planted more than 1,000 churches in northwest Congo with 40,000 members. Forty-five missionaries served a region the size of England, which was home to three major tribal groups: the Longando-speaking Bongando tribe at Yoseki, with two hundred churches and 18,000 believers; the Ngombe tribe at Munda, Bosodjafo and Lulonga; and the Mongo, covering Bondandanga, Baringa, Ikau, Basankusu and Yuli-Mpenzele. To provide integration and cohesion for hundreds of isolated churches, the Community of the Association of Evangelical Churches of the Lulonga (CADELU) was formed. At the time of independence CADELU churches were 'mostly self-supporting and self-governing, and to a certain extent, self-propagating. Pastors were functioning and evangelists were living in bush villages, touring the scattered churches to teach and advise.'

Baringa

With Shaumba's burden resting on them to deepen the faith and Biblical knowledge of believers, Audrey and Elleea left for Baringa. Baringa was a hospital station, so medical staff and Mike Wide, their field supervisor, were already living there when they arrived. After independence, the hostility between tribes, suppressed for years, had begun to resurface in some areas and undermined much of what the missionaries had previously taught; so there was a need to re-establish the work, primarily in the field of training and Bible teaching. Audrey and Elleea began with a school for the catechist teachers from all the different tribes to strengthen their Bible knowledge, which could then be imparted to their people. This school was later upgraded to become the Baringa Institute of Theology, which fell under the auspices of Action Partners in 1999. They also had a vision to establish a secondary school and a Bible school

The Maringa River at Baringa beach. The Mongo people made their own canoes.

for pastors and evangelists, which were established in the mid 1960s.

They advised all the pastors about the new catechist school and asked them to mention any Christian men in their areas who felt the call of God to be village teachers or evangelists. They also promoted the school at the pastors' assembly meetings.

The new catechist school

Before the start of the term the students arrived in dribs and drabs to build their own mud houses in which they were to board throughout the academic year, which began in September and went through to June. When the term started in the autumn of 1961 twenty or thirty men had enrolled. Their wives and families, who were considered a 'stabilizing influence' for the men, came along too.

The catechist training was for two years initially; it was later raised for the training of pastors. Sometimes the village teachers became pastors after five or six years of training, but only after being thoroughly vetted by their local pastor and elders. There was an annual intake of students, and after a few years, white and Congolese teachers, who had been through the school, joined the staff.

Most village women were completely illiterate, so Audrey gave them basic teaching in literacy in the early morning, before they started work in the fields. Many of the children were enthusiastic in their studies and were soon able to recite passages of Scripture.

Elizabeth Pritchard, writing in 1973, said that whole families left the school and returned to their villages 'with a deeper knowledge of the Bible and their minds sharpened by study to "try the spirits". They will be a bulwark against resurgent heathen religions and superstitions which are now sweeping the villages.'

Congolese pastors

The Featherstones supported the village teacher/evangelists,

School building within the Baringa *lifeta*

who were each responsible for twenty or so villages, visiting them continually to introduce people to the gospel. These men had a vital work to teach the basics of the Christian faith to their fellow tribesmen, and to help them grasp that Jesus died to save his people from their sins and to deliver them from God's anger. When a group was converted, the pastor was responsible for their spiritual growth and discipleship.

Those pastors who knew the word of God well made numerous cross-references in their sermons. Audrey remembered one of the Congolese pastors preaching when suddenly, in the middle of his sermon, he picked on one of the congregation to supply him with a Scripture verse or reference! Whenever Audrey passed the pastors' houses, she frequently saw them studying the Bible.

The pastors and church leaders met together annually to discuss their work and the members of their churches. Church discipline was an important matter. For the glory of God, a close watch was kept on how the disciples of Christ were living: were they getting drunk, were husbands and wives always arguing, were they attending church? It was easy to observe everyone in the village, for life was lived out in the open, not behind closed doors as in the West. Everyone knew what was going on, and any bad behaviour was reported. If a man or woman was living in a way that brought dishonour to the name of Christ, they were disciplined by being put out of fellowship and denied communion. When they repented, they were welcomed back.

In the seekers' classes, those who wanted to become Christians were told that fetishes must be destroyed and alcohol was forbidden. If a tribal chief became a Christian, he was not only exhorted to have only one wife, but encouraged to allow his other wives to return to their villages in order to find another husband, and to reach a settlement with their families over dowries.

At this point all seemed to be going well. The building work was progressing, and the training, secondary and Bible schools were up and running. Since independence, every mission station had an intercom and at a set time each day Audrey and

Elleea preaching at a Baringa church service

Elleea made contact with other stations — a contact that was to prove vital in the days ahead. The U.N. had pulled out of Congo because they believed everything was now on an even keel and the various missionary organizations looked forward to a time of consolidation. Little did they foresee the destructive atrocities that were about to sweep across the land.

Field treasurer

RBMU had around twelve schools in the whole of their mission area and each school had classroom teachers. Back in 1960 the central government had agreed to subsidize the teachers' salaries with a family allowance, and in order to oversee the payment of these monies, Audrey, whose bank experience was considered useful, was asked to take on the role of field treasurer. She had to send the government a list of all the teachers, their qualifications and the number of children in their families, which determined the size of the allowance each received. Audrey found the whole exercise a 'nightmare' as there were so many 'extended' families, making it almost impossible to keep track of which children belonged to which family.

Every three months she submitted a return to the government, who then sent a cheque, which she tried to cash so the teachers could be paid. Cashing a cheque was not easy, as there were no banks; so Audrey found a trader, who was willing to cash the cheque for Congolese francs. This meant she had to carry around thousands of francs on her own person! Having sought out reliable messengers, she tried to get the money safely to each school. Often someone from a particular school came and asked for the money. At other times she was accused of not handing out enough money. 'You have only paid me for two children — I now have five!' exclaimed an exasperated teacher. Not only was it difficult to verify individual claims, but the number of children often increased (fathers adopted nephews and nieces to secure more money) between sending off the returns and receiving the cheque — a problem not helped by the government's procrastination.

Often Audrey was not believed when she said the money due had not yet come from the government. One day when

Audrey giving the treasurer's report at a conference (held in her house)

she walked out of her office she saw a placard pinned to the door which said: 'War department — keep out!' Mike Wide had placed it there as he knew some of the problems Audrey was enduring.

A frightening journey

Once, their legal representative, Sebo Baoitti, had to go down to Leopoldville on business and he asked Audrey, as field treasurer, to join him there in order to sort out a financial problem a school was experiencing. Audrey left Basankusu in a very small plane. A pilot and about a dozen Congolese were on board, plus their chickens and goats. They had not been flying very long when Audrey noticed what looked like a large grey ruler stretching across the sky — a storm was approaching and they were about to fly straight into it.

Suddenly, there was a 'most horrendous bang' from underneath the plane, so loud that Audrey thought the whole floor was about to disintegrate. The plane wobbled violently from side to side. Both Audrey and the Congolese were absolutely terrified as they imagined the plane was breaking up. The pilot, looking like a ghost, left his cockpit and started to inspect the floor. All Audrey could think of was Elleea back at base. 'Will I see him again?' she whispered to herself. Then they hit the storm, with gale force winds and lightning, and a buffeting they only just survived. To cap it all, after this first storm, as they were coming into Coquilhatville, Audrey to her horror saw another storm brewing, which tossed the small plane around for another half an hour.

The passengers never did find out what had caused the bang, but they eventually landed safely, for which Audrey praised God. They were told, however, that the plane had to undergo an inspection and, much to their relief, another was provided for their passage to Leopoldville.

After Audrey had struggled with the role of field treasurer for three or four years, a Swiss man was asked to take over until the Congolese were trained — much to Audrey's delight.

16
The Simba rebellion

Before continuing the Featherstones' story, it will be helpful to examine an uprising that played a significant part in their lives as well as in the history of Congo and its church.

****

A summary

A turning point in Congolese politics came late in 1962, when the U.N. moved from being a neutral peacekeeping force to active intervention against Katanga. After strong initial resistance, the Katangan army surrendered in January 1963 and Tshombe fled to Spain, although his exile did not end his involvement in Congo. President Kasavubu, faced in 1964 with serious unrest in the eastern provinces, attempted to restore peace by inviting Tshombe to return from exile as the nation's prime minister. New elections for the national assembly were held in April 1965 and Tshombe's party appeared to win a majority, but in the aftermath of the election, Kasavubu dismissed him from his post. Tshombe returned to Spain, leaving Congo in political chaos.

The Simba rebellion

The central figures behind the 1964 eastern rebellion were Christophe Gbenye, a radical former member of Gizenga's Parti Solidaire Africain (PSA), and Gaston Soumialot, who had been sent to Burundi by the Conseil National de Liberation (CNL), a left-wing political movement based in the former French Congo, with the task of organizing the uprising. Soumialot had recruited thousands of dedicated supporters, who were dissatisfied with the brutality, corruption and incompetence of the central Congolese government. Many of the rebels were animists and many believed that 'magic water' dispensed by witch doctors could make a warrior immune to government bullets, transforming them into a 'Simba' (Swahili for 'lion'). Consequently, the Congolese rebellion became known as the Simba rebellion.

The Simba rebellion, which affected Kivu and Orientale provinces, quickly gained ground. In August, the Soumialot forces, under the new name of the National Liberation Army (Armée Nationale de Libération — ANL), captured Stanleyville, where they set up a rebel government. Equipped with weapons left by the routed Congolese National Army, the Simbas pushed north and west of Stanleyville, eventually penetrating as far west as Lisala on the Congo River.

By 5 September almost half of Congo and seven out of twenty-one local capitals were in rebel hands; but as the rebel movement spread, discipline became more difficult to maintain, and acts of violence and terror increased. Thirty-four Protestant missionaries, as well as several children, met a violent death. While no RBMU missionaries lost their lives, property losses for affected missions amounted to millions of pounds. Three hundred whites and 'tens of thousands of Congolese' were massacred, including government officials, political leaders of opposition parties, provincial and local police, schoolteachers, and others believed to have been westernized. One reporter observed that Congo was 'virtually ungovernable'.

In its rivalry with the Soviet Union, the United States had committed itself to the support of the central Congolese government, and the C.I.A. began to organize a small air force to support the Congolese ground forces in their war against the Simbas; but despite the C.I.A.'s involvement, the rebellion continued to spread. In a move of desperation, the Congolese government recalled Moise Tshombe from exile and again made him prime minister, with a mandate to end the regional revolts. The U.S. government agreed to help Tshombe raise a force of mercenaries to fight the Simbas, and to expand its air strikes. The Simbas had no anti-aircraft guns or aircraft to oppose these attacks, and the effectiveness of the U.S. air force was aided by the general incompetence and indiscipline of the rebel forces as a fighting unit.

The rebellion quashed

As he set about the task of quashing the rebellion, Tshombe relied on the Katangan gendarmes, recalled from exile in Angola, and a few hundred battle-hardened white mercenaries. The former were immediately integrated into the Congolese National Army, with the latter providing much-needed leadership for the conduct of military operations against Simba forces. Supported by air strikes, these units spearheaded attacks against rebel strongholds. As the white mercenaries took the offensive and, with their technical superiority and discipline, began to recapture rebel strongholds, the fighting grew progressively more brutal. Numerous atrocities were committed.

Mercenary elements played a decisive role in retaking Lisala, Boende and Kindu, by which time the revolutionary government in Stanleyville had decided to hold local European residents hostage, in the hope of using them as bargaining chips in negotiations with the central authorities. Several hundred hostages were taken to Stanleyville and placed under guard in the Victoria Hotel.

Operation Dragon Rouge

The rebels' action resulted in the joint Belgian-American parachute rescue operation on Stanleyville, on 24 November, scheduled to coincide with the arrival of the Congolese National Army and mercenary units in the vicinity of the provincial capital. A squadron of aircraft dropped over 300 Belgian paratroopers at Stanleyville airport. After securing the airfield and clearing the runway, the paratroopers made their way to the hotel, where they prevented Simbas from killing the hostages, whom they evacuated via the airfield. Over the next two days over 1,800 Americans and Europeans were evacuated as well as around 300 Congolese.

The capture of Stanleyville dealt a devastating blow to the rebels. The two key rebel leaders, Gbenye and Soumialot, fled to Cairo. Demoralization quickly set in among the Simbas, and by December, the eastern rebellion was reduced to isolated pockets of resistance.

By the end of 1965, the Simba rebellion was essentially over, although some mopping-up actions continued for over a year afterwards. Tshombe, whose success in quelling the Simba revolt was overshadowed by the joint Belgian/U.S.A. operation, became involved in a power struggle with President Kasavubu, which led to a constitutional deadlock. Tshombe was charged with treason and again fled to Spain.

Mobutu

Joseph-Desire Mobutu (later Mobutu Sese Seko), a military officer who had exercised control from behind the scenes earlier in the 1960s and an avowed anti-communist, with the help of the C.I.A., seized power once again in a military coup on 25 November 1965, and became supreme head of state. The new regime, which became one of the most dictatorial and corrupt, received considerable initial approval from other African countries and from the United States, who saw him as an ally against communism in Africa.

Mobutu established a one party state and called for a return to 'African authenticity'. He banned all other political organizations, and religious services were forbidden on national days. Christian organizations — Christianity was regarded as a white man's religion and therefore 'incompatible with African indigenization' — were ordered not to pray for him or the government. Even the use of Christian first names was suppressed. Despite the country's obvious natural resources, including copper, gold and diamonds, the Congolese continued to sink further into poverty and the economy soon collapsed. Mobutu amassed a personal fortune estimated to be as much as five billion dollars, while the country's infrastructure built up from the colonial period was left to decay.

Mobutu Sese Seko in the 1960s sporting his trademark leopardskin

Many pastors remained strong through the storm at great personal cost. Pastor Benjamin Lofinda at Ikau urged his fellow believers to distance themselves from the hysterical nationalism that possessed many and as a result he was branded unpatriotic and a traitor, and bitterly accused of bias towards the missionaries, 'a daunting accusation at a time when all around the cry was going up — "Africa for the Africans"'. Anyone adhering to former church policies was called a 'tool of the white man', but Lofinda stood by what he believed to be the best for his people, even though he knew that in other districts some pastors had been hounded and murdered for their stand.

Simon Mokala, a quiet, humble man of the Ngombe, who had risen from the post of village teacher to pastor-in-chief of the Bopengi section of the Lulonga church, endured severe persecution 'with all the grace and meekness that only Christ can give'. Sadly not everyone remained faithful.

****

With the above history of the Simba rebellion in mind, we are now ready to examine the troubles from the Featherstones' perspective and to see how it affected their lives and missionary service.

17
Time to escape

The Simbas' aim

Although the work was progressing well at Baringa, the Featherstones and their colleagues began to hear rumours of an uprising down at Kasai, southeast of where they were situated. They heard that witchcraft and magic were being used against innocent people and that leaders were telling young men, who were flocking to join the ranks of the rebellion, that they were invincible and immune to the bullets of their enemies — a message believed by the gullible masses. 'We are going to be authentic Africans. We want to be like we were before the white people came to our country', was the leaders' battle cry.

They heard, from reliable sources, that the Simbas wanted to destroy hospitals, schools and anything to do with colonization, which of course included missionaries. Over the years of the twentieth century, missionaries had been in the forefront of education, medical work, and the spread of Christianity, and therefore anyone, including the Congolese, who worked in a school, hospital or church, was a target. The Featherstones did not want to believe a report that claimed even small children were involved in burning pastors' houses and destroying anything to do with western civilization. The Congolese army, already weak and disorganized, was terrified of the Simbas' witchcraft and magic, and too afraid to intervene. As the rebellion gained momentum, Audrey's heart sank as she realized that many of those involved had been brought up in the mission schools.

Escape

At first Audrey and Elleea tried to ignore the rumours and carried on with their work as normal. Since independence they were in close radio contact with other stations, and heard from them that the rebellion had swept into Stanleyville and was turning west towards their area. It was apparent that no one could stop the rebels. The village people had already fled deep into the forest.

When it was reported that the Simbas were approaching Yoseki, Audrey and Elleea, and their fellow missionaries, knew they were in direct line of the rebels. They heard that Arthur and Elizabeth Wright had fled Yoseki and were on their way to join them at Baringa; they then knew that escape was the only sensible option. The Congolese pastor and elders of the church joined with Audrey, Elleea, the Wrights and one or two others to pray for God's guidance and protection. 'You know how much we love you and you love us,' the pastor and elders said, 'but in one sense if you stay, you are a liability to us. We will abandon everything and hide deep in the forest. We want you to get out while you can.'

Shortly before their decision to leave, Audrey had cashed a cheque from the government for the teachers' salaries, which meant she had put tens of thousands of francs into the mission safe. 'What are we going to do with all this money?' she asked. They did not want the Simbas to get their hands on it so they decided to seal it in hundreds of paper packages. They then prayed with their Congolese friends and said, '*Elaka nko nzakomba*', which means, 'Whatever God wills, we are in his hands. We trust him.' They hugged each other and, with tears streaming down their faces, said, 'May we all meet again, but if not, we will meet up there,' pointing to the heavens.

While the missionaries were saying farewell, they received another urgent radio message telling them to leave without delay while the road was still open, for the Simbas (thousands of them) were only about 100 miles away. (Most of them were travelling on foot, but some drove vehicles.) They hurriedly packed their Land Rover with a few belongings, spreading the packets of money on the front seat and covering them with a

Elleea saying goodbye to the church leaders at Baringa

A final hug for Audrey as she leaves Baringa

rug. Arthur drove and Audrey and Elizabeth sat beside him in the front, with Elleea in the back; so the four of them started the hazardous 150-mile journey to Ikau and Basankusu, where there was an airstrip.

They crossed many streams on their journey, but the only way to cross one of the main rivers was via a Bailey bridge. Every so often soldiers stopped them and, with guns pointing at them, demanded money. Arthur and Elleea stood patiently outside the vehicle, talking to them in their own language, while Audrey and Elizabeth remained inside smiling innocently at the soldiers and sitting on all the packets of francs. As they waited they prayed earnestly that the Lord would restrain the soldiers from searching their vehicle. Eventually the armed men gave up and sent them on their way.

Stopped in their tracks

They arrived in Basankusu in the middle of the night and met up with Sebo and Mali Baoitti. The British embassy had sent word via the intercom that they were sending a plane up from Leopoldville for the purpose of evacuation. The airfield was about five miles out of Basankusu, and the next day they heard news that a small plane was about to land. They started to drive out of Basankusu, but were stopped by a group of twenty young soldiers, who surrounded the Land Rover and with menacing looks demanded a bribe. The four missionaries were determined not to give them anything, and refused to allow them to search their belongings.

Throughout the uneasy stand off, which lasted about three hours, the missionaries tried to talk to the men about the Lord Jesus Christ, until at last the sergeant snapped, 'Let them go!' They did not need to be told twice and hurried to the airfield, hoping the plane from Leopoldville had not already departed. When they arrived, the officials said, 'We thought you weren't coming. Get in quick!' And so, with all the money intact, they jumped on board. They took off immediately and flew down to Leopoldville. Audrey remembered thinking that both the pilot and co-pilot were a bit too relaxed, chatting and drinking coffee, with feet up — flying the plane seemed secondary, but they arrived safely.

Atrocities

On arrival in Leopoldville, they were taken into the centre of the town, where there were literally hundreds of missionaries assembled ready to be evacuated from Congo. The embassy arranged for them to stay at a house in the town. They met other missionaries from different organizations who had escaped from Stanleyville, and it was from them that they heard about atrocities at the hands of the Simbas. There were harrowing tales about how many of their colleagues had been massacred, and stories of looting, pillaging and rape. A Canadian missionary was absolutely distraught — his wife had been elsewhere when the order came to evacuate and he had left without her. He had no idea what had happened to her. Audrey heard later that she was found alive and well.

The Simba rebels swept through RBMU's area, destroying almost everything in their path. They arrived at Baringa, searching for medical help and supplies, but the Congolese nurses had hidden the new shipment of drugs in the hospital ceiling. No one was killed at Baringa, but only 200 miles away at Boende, hundreds were massacred and thrown into the river.

At Mompono houses were burned and one elderly and faithful Congolese pastor, who continued to visit from village to village, even after the Simbas had arrived, was caught, tied to a tree, and asked, 'What money have you got, old man?' All he had were a few coins, which the village Christians had given him. The Simbas shot him and threw his body into the river. Another man was cut down as he rode his bike to a preaching point. When a RBMU doctor returned to the area, a group of women came onto the porch of his house. The leader of the group was the elderly wife of the pastor who had been shot. She wanted to sing a hymn of praise to God for his grace and love to her, even in the midst of tragedy.

The return to Baringa

The Featherstones and the Wrights stayed in Leopoldville for several weeks. By this time the central government had called for the assistance of mercenaries, who were pushing the Simbas back. The village people helped halt the Simbas' advance by destroying the Bailey bridge, halfway between Baringa and Basankusu. Once the Simbas realized they were up against foreign mercenaries, their sense of invincibility vanished and they turned tail and fled. Their original intention had been to reach Leopoldville and to take over the whole country, but in this they failed.

While Audrey, Elleea and the Wrights were in Leopoldville, word came via the embassy that the government wanted three or four missionaries to return to their stations. The mercenaries had been able to push the Simbas back to beyond Baringa and to gain control of many villages. However, the villagers were still absolutely terrified and hiding deep in the forest, refusing to return to their homes. The thinking behind the government's request was that if people saw their missionaries, they would have confidence to leave the forest and re-occupy their homes. Audrey, Elleea and the Wrights decided to fly back from Leopoldville to Ikau.

Because the Bailey bridge had been destroyed, they secured a canoe with a somewhat unreliable outboard motor, and chugged and paddled the 100 miles or so up river towards Baringa, without any Congolese help. To make the most of the daylight hours, they left at 3:00 a.m., with the sun rising at about 4:30 a.m. They travelled all that day, and when the sun finally sank at about 6:00 p.m., the only light they had to find their way was from a small hurricane lamp. It was dark and eerie. Although they knew the mercenaries had pushed back the Simbas beyond Baringa, they had no idea if some were still hiding on the banks of the river or in the forest.

They arrived at Baringa at about 11:00 p.m., wondering what awaited them. They had been away for some seven to eight weeks. They climbed out of the canoe and made their way to the mission station, passing Congolese soldiers, who were now occupying the missionaries' houses with their many

The Bailey Bridge

wives and mistresses. They were roasting meat, the sight and smell of which was 'absolutely vile'. They were not pleased to see the missionaries.

The exhausted missionaries then walked the four or five miles from the mission station to the leper camp (the *lifeta*) deep in the forest. (When the government had initiated the policy that lepers should, as far as possible, be treated in their own homes, the number of lepers at Baringa had fallen from a thousand at one point to about a hundred. The missionaries were therefore able to establish an educational centre using some of the redundant buildings. Audrey and Elleea's house was also within the camp.)

They arrived at the camp and were greeted enthusiastically by the lepers, who told them that when the Simbas had arrived at Baringa, they searched all over the mission station before asking the few people left, 'Where does that path go?'

'To the leper camp,' came the reply. The soldiers were too scared to go near it; so the educational centre, the missionaries' homes and all the equipment belonging to the mission in the *lifeta* were protected.

The Congolese soldiers were reluctant to leave the houses, but eventually, on the orders of the mercenaries, they agreed and the hospital station was able to reopen.

Getting back to normal

For the next few weeks they gradually settled back into some sort of routine, with much of their time taken up in clearing the 'disgusting mess' left by the soldiers. The hospital and most of the buildings needed a thorough cleaning. Audrey and Elleea were still nervous at night because they did not know if the Simbas were close by, intent on murdering them. They felt much happier when they heard that the mercenaries had pushed the Simbas eastward towards Yoseki, where Arthur and Elizabeth had run the hospital. With news of the rebels' retreat filtering through, and to the delight of the missionaries, people slowly but surely emerged from the forest.

Much needed supplies of food and medicines were given to the villagers who had been trapped in the forest for weeks.

The Land Rover was quickly repaired and Audrey, Elleea and the Wrights set about visiting various mission stations such as Mompono and Yoseki, stopping off at the villages along the way. As they travelled, village after village, which they had previously visited in the course of their pastoral and evangelistic work, lay in ruins, with only a few survivors brave enough to show themselves.

One of the problems they encountered was actually reaching the villages with the Land Rover. Baringa was on the south side of the Maringa River and the only means of crossing it was on an old barge; so they had to manoeuvre the Land Rover carefully onto the barge, with its wheels teetering on the edge.

Once, on their return, they found that the barge had sunk. Unsure of what to do, they discovered that a courier boat that had sailed upriver full of soldiers was docked nearby. After securing a place on board, they drove the Land Rover onto the deck. The boat was squalid and overcrowded with Congolese and soldiers. The captain, who resented their presence, grudgingly offered them a filthy cabin.

That evening, while they were sailing downstream to Baringa, they noticed that the deck was covered with huge white maggots and there was a terrible smell of rotting flesh. 'Where are the maggots coming from?' they asked themselves, as they wondered how they were going to cope with the stench for the next three days. Eventually they found out that the soldiers had been killing monkeys and other animals upriver, and had stacked the carcasses in the front two cabins, where they had been rotting for the last four or five days. Their sense of disgust was heightened as they watched the soldiers eating the maggot-infested meat.

On their travels, when Audrey and Elleea arrived at a large village, they called out, 'Is anyone there?' Then they sang a hymn. After a few minutes faces began to appear in the forest, and when the villagers realized that the missionaries had returned, they came streaming out. They all embraced and cried, and the villagers could hardly believe that their friends were still alive. More harrowing stories of massacres and imprisonments were related. Then they asked, 'Please, please, have

A courier boat at Baringa beach

you brought us some Bibles? All these weeks we have been in the forest and the rain has ruined our Bibles. We need more Bibles!'

With the help of the missionaries, the villagers started to rebuild their homes and their lives.

What did the church learn?

The Simba rebellion was a severe test for the Congolese church. Some Christians were murdered because of their faith, others because they opposed the cruelty of the rebels, still others for their education or their western dress; and yet, by the grace and goodness of God, the church grew. Those who hid in the forest experienced the presence of Christ in a deeper way and depended on his grace more fully. Pastors started to preach and witness with greater boldness and power. A Mompono nurse and pastoral assistant, whose testimony is representative of many, declared: 'I was completely alone for three weeks [as he hid from the rebels]. God taught me to pray. Before the trouble we used to think of "things" as everything — as he pointed to a radio and a lamp — but we had to abandon all and God taught us the important thing is eternal life.'

Another leader said, 'After independence when the Simbas came, I thought God could have stopped this. I saw people killed and stuffed in sacks. But God saw we were too proud and inflated since independence, and God taught us we must look to him.' The resentment that had developed in many Congolese Christian hearts soon disappeared, and as was seen with the Featherstones, they welcomed the missionaries back — they danced in the streets, waved flags, sang hymns and hugged and kissed them. Even local government officials went out of their way to greet them. The Congolese church had survived through the darkest storm.

18
New beginnings

When the four missionaries arrived at Yoseki, Arthur and Elizabeth received a tremendous welcome from the people. However, the rebels had ransacked their home. Arthur was a talented musician and his piano had been shipped out to Congo years before. He went to look for it, but could not find it. He was then told that the Simbas had taken out the strings and used them to trap animals, while the body of the piano had been hacked to pieces.

Striking testimonies

Audrey and Elleea spent two or three weeks in Yoseki, helping to put things right and hearing the stories of rampaging Simbas. The hospital work never managed to restart because of insufficient staff, but the church continued to grow. Audrey remembered that during the weeks she was there, the drums could be heard so clearly because of the station's slightly higher position. At church on Sunday morning, the pastor read out all the meetings for the following week and the names of the people who would lead them. Early each morning there was a women's meeting in the main church for prayer and Bible Study, and later in the day there was a meeting for men.

While it was still dark, with mist rising from the forest floor, Audrey and Elizabeth got up and went to the women's devotions. They were thrilled at the sight of fifty or sixty women gathered together to hear the Bible taught and to engage in a time of prayer. Their testimonies and courage amazed them. In the face of such harrowing experiences with the Simbas, they were still

Elleea and Audrey (1965)

able to praise God. 'When we were hiding in the forest,' they enthused, 'we were afraid our children would start crying and let the Simbas know where we were, but God protected us!'

One woman told Audrey how her husband had been massacred, and then said, 'You know what it says in the Psalms about the palm tree reaching out until it finds water. Other trees are destroyed, but the palm tree bends and does not break. This is what God has done. We are not broken despite the massacre.' Again and again these Congolese women, even in their deepest sorrows, testified to the goodness of God and his divine protection. They had such a simple but strong faith, and a deep hunger for the Word of God. When missionaries finally left, the work continued to prosper in the hands of good Congolese pastors and elders.

A Bible conference

The mission station at Yoseki sought to reach out to the Bongando tribe, who spoke the Longando language. Before independence the missionaries at Yoseki had held a big three-day Bible teaching conference each year for their people and Elleea was often invited to give the main address. It was quite an event, with between one and two thousand people attending. On account of the numbers, it was always held outdoors in front of a large anthill, which served as the pulpit. Many of those who attended walked for miles to be there. Very often, at the conclusion of the conference, people who had come under conviction of sin, brought out their charms and fetishes, made a big pile and burned them. Sadly, these conferences were never resurrected after the Simba rebellion.

Schools

Yoseki had a separate school for boys and girls, who used slates for reading and writing. In the early days, when the Featherstones started establishing schools to educate children, they were always for boys, although they encouraged girls to attend too. The villagers thought it unnecessary for girls to be educated, because by the age of seven or eight they were

The church at the *lifeta*, where the Featherstones worshipped each Sunday

Inside the church at the *lifeta*. (The seats were concrete benches, so they could be scrubbed.) Audrey cannot be seen, but she was probably sitting next to Elleea (bottom right) near the wall to give some support to her back during a long service!

A ward service at Baringa hospital (August 1964)

ICM Bible School within the *lifeta* at Baringa (1966)

expected to help in their parents' gardens, which families relied on for food. The mother carried a huge basket on her back or head, along with a baby in a sling, and the girl carried the tools; so understandably it was difficult to persuade villagers to let their girls attend school instead of helping them.

Some of the girls managed to go to school. During the 1950/60s, RBMU had established two or three good boarding schools for girls as the people realized that girls as well as boys needed to grow up knowing how to read and write. There was no boarding school for girls at Baringa, but classes were held for village girls who wanted to join in. There were large boarding schools at Yoseki, Ikau and other mission stations.

Eventually one of the men was given a sewing machine and he made school uniforms for the boys and girls. One poor boy, desperately in need of a uniform, was one day working away with his knife, cutting grass and cleaning the paths. He was wearing a pair of ragged shorts and a vest, which was not much more than a few pieces of string around him. Not only was he uncomfortable, but the vest was impeding his work. Audrey asked him, 'You look as though you need a new vest. Wouldn't it be better for you if you took it off?'

In astonishment, he replied, 'Do you expect me to go naked?'

New beginnings

After an exhausting journey to the small mission station at Njafa, where there were no missionaries living, the Featherstones and Wrights were greeted by large numbers of enthusiastic villagers. Although it was late at night, they conducted a short service before crawling into bed in their mud hut. At about 4:00 a.m., Audrey was awoken by a soft drumbeat. She climbed out of bed and peered through the window into the darkness. She saw first one person and then another walking out of their houses, womenfolk, making their way to the village church. The drums stopped and then the women started singing. Audrey realized they were having a prayer meeting before going into the forest to tend their gardens, where they worked for the rest of the day. None of the missionaries had taught them to pray in this way.

Typical village mothers and children of the Mongo tribe

Audrey asked them, 'Why do you pray so early in the morning?'

'Don't you remember after Jesus was crucified and they put him in the grave,' they replied, 'the women went there looking for him but he wasn't there. They thought he was dead but he wasn't! They got up early to meet with Jesus. We are following their example.'

After two or three weeks of visiting the mission stations and trying to ascertain needs — many of the gardens had been ruined by the Simbas, and Bibles and hymn books destroyed by the weather — the Featherstones realized that the best way to help was to acquire everyday supplies such as flour, sugar and dried milk for the villagers, and from that point the work of rebuilding progressed more rapidly.

By the latter months of 1964, things were beginning to get shipshape again. 1965 was a particularly fruitful year, especially for Audrey and Elleea at Baringa, because a new kind of work was developing. A Bible school and secondary school were established and educationalists joined the team, such as the disciplined yet humorous Joyce Ferguson. New buildings were erected within the confines of the leper colony and many young men, who had been through the primary system, advanced into secondary education. (Initially, some of the young folk were afraid of the lepers, but their prejudices soon disappeared.) There was a sense of 'new beginnings', and all felt great encouragement.

Fire!

In 1965 a near disaster struck. At the back of their small house within the *lifeta* at Baringa, Audrey and Elleea had a cookhouse and behind that was a storeroom where they kept trunks, tinned food and 200 litre drums of kerosene, petrol and paraffin for their lamps. One evening, just before 6:00 p.m., Elleea was lighting the lamps as he always did. The paraffin was low so he went to the storeroom with a small hurricane lamp and a container into which to pour some fuel for the lamp in the house. As he tipped the drum on its side, some paraffin splashed onto his clothes and onto the hurricane lamp, which immediately ignited. Flames soon engulfed Elleea's only means of escape, the storeroom door.

Meanwhile Audrey was sitting at home wondering why her husband was taking so long. She stepped outside and to her horror saw huge flames shooting out of the storehouse and up into the darkness. She rushed towards the door, but could not open it. Apart from the devouring noise of the flames everything was quiet as it always was at that time of the day. People were in their houses eating their meal and were 250 yards away. All she could do was to cry out to the Lord.

Just at that moment, three students came walking up the path; they were going to a missionary's house to have a time of prayer together and to talk over their next day's assignments. As soon as they saw the flames they rushed over crying, 'Where is Botuli?'

'He's trapped inside there!' shouted Audrey, pointing to the storehouse. Immediately the three boys ran to the back of the store. They hauled each other onto the roof, made a hole in it and leaning down called out to Elleea. Apart from praying and getting as far away as possible from the fire, Elleea had not been able to do anything to help himself. When the boys leaned through the hole, Elleea saw them, climbed on a box and lifted his hands for them to haul him out. Amazingly he only had one or two superficial burns. The whole storehouse was soon completely gutted. Thankfully the fire did not spread or reach the house, as Audrey had only just cashed in a cheque to pay the schoolteachers!

Elsa Morgan, who had appeared on the scene during the rescue, did her best to comfort Audrey in her distress. As everyone was busy removing things from the house in case the fire spread, a shout went up because a local woman was stealing Audrey's curtains. She was caught, but Elsa was shocked that anyone could do such a thing in the middle of a potential disaster.

News of the fire reached Mike Wide, who dressed Elleea's burns. Audrey was in shock for two or three days, but grateful to God that he had sent rescuers to save her husband.

Educationalists

Although RMBU had managed to secure its funds and property before independence, it had not, according to the educationalist Joan Sledmere, equipped the church 'to meet the new dangers of the day; we had left them almost totally unequipped to obey Christ's commands to heal the sick [there were no Congolese doctors] and unable to cope with the rising demand among the young for better education'. After independence many of Congo's youth left their forest homes for the cities in search of better education and economic opportunities. 'With this migration, the old Congo of the Guinness era passed into history and with it the effectiveness of the old approaches to mission.' The Roman Catholics shrewdly constructed Lovanium University in Leopoldville, which assured them of 'dominance in the new nation'.

As new missionaries arrived, they set up secondary schools and teacher training establishments, and the focus of attention shifted from evangelism to secular teaching. The language medium of the educationalists was French. In a few short years everything seemed to change. The older missionaries retired, while the new missionaries, who had come essentially to do secondary school work, gradually trained the Congolese to take over the work. During the 1970s, for one reason or another, the educationalists left. Joyce Ferguson, for example, went to work in French Congo for a time. In a way, the work was rightly handed over to the Congolese, which was what Audrey and Elleea had always strived to achieve, but they also realized that missionaries with a good grasp of the native tongue were still needed to teach the word of God more deeply to the growing church.

19
Home — for the last time?

Health problems

For their latest term the Featherstones had been out on the field since 1961, and by early 1966 Elleea, who was then in his early sixties and had been in Congo since 1933, was not in the best of health. Audrey had begun to notice small signs that his health was deteriorating. His usual vitality was missing; one or two rodent ulcers and skin cancers appeared on his face and elsewhere; and when he was preaching, he sometimes used the wrong word or mispronounced a word, which was not at all like him, for he had such a good grasp of the language. She thought he was just tired, and put it down to a long and difficult stretch in Congo, which had included the stress of the Simba rebellion.

Arthur and Elizabeth Wright also noticed a deterioration in Elleea and suggested, 'You both need a good break, especially Elleea — and he must get those skin cancers examined; but we can't bear to think you might not be back again.' (Audrey and Elleea had discussed retirement with their friends.) Preparing to return home, the Featherstones wondered if they were leaving Congo for good. The future was uncertain.

The journey home

The time came for them to leave for furlough. Their journey took them overland from Baringa to Boende, a government post, where they picked up the courier boat to Mbandaka (Coquilhatville). From there they booked to go down to

Leopoldville on the passenger riverboat, which had the luxury of cabins and a dining room. As they were preparing to board the *Reineastrid*, with several suitcases in their hands, the customs soldiers looked at them suspiciously and, with guns pointing in their direction, snapped, 'What's in your cases? Have you any diamonds?'

'Only clothing and papers,' they replied. Such a response did not satisfy the soldiers, who made them empty everything onto the pavement. They poked around in all their possessions and subjected them to fierce interrogation. Finally they were allowed to put everything back. With thanks to God ringing in their hearts, they climbed on board, found their cabin, and started the journey to Leopoldville. They enjoyed being on the main river, with its huge islands.

The boat docked at certain places en route, one of which was the BMS mission station at Bolobo. As always, missionaries came down to the boat for their letters. When they saw Audrey and Elleea, they invited them to their station, which was similar to the station at Baringa, and told them that Grace Lowman was going to join them on their journey. Grace had been a friend for years and they were delighted with the news. After a quick meal, they returned to the boat. Elleea was very tired, but Grace looked closely at Audrey and cried, 'You look awful!' She then produced a small bottle of brandy and gave Audrey a tot. It really picked her up!

They eventually arrived at Leopoldville, where Grace left them. Audrey and Elleea were kept behind and again the soldiers wanted to check their identity. Their cases were emptied for a second time and they were asked again if they had any diamonds. 'How can we have diamonds?' they answered somewhat impatiently. 'We are missionaries. We have come from the equatorial province — diamonds are down in Katanga.' The soldiers, paranoid about white people carrying diamonds, were not satisfied and marched Elleea off for questioning. Audrey was left alone. At last, after two hours, he was escorted back. Grudgingly the soldiers allowed them to put their things back in the cases.

Audrey and Elleea in a canoe (1966). From front to back: Ruth Petersen (missionary with Disciples of Christ), Elleea, Audrey, Elizabeth Wright and Arthur Wright.

Mercenaries or missionaries?

They arrived at the Union mission house in the town and spent a couple of days there before catching the only train that day from Leopoldville to Matadi. Educated Congolese were also travelling, but in their carriage they were the only white people. They sat in their seats, relieved to be on their way.

What they were unaware of, however, was the tension that then existed between hundreds of mercenaries, who had helped liberate Congo from the Simbas, and the government. By 1966 the mercenaries had completed the 'mopping up exercise' and were demanding their money. 'Now, where is our pay? If you don't pay us the money you owe us, there will be trouble' — a threat that was not received kindly by the government, who sent out word, 'If you see any mercenaries, arrest them!'

The journey to Matadi should have taken twelve hours, but after about six hours the train came to an abrupt halt. Suddenly there was banging on the door of the carriage. The local gendarmerie entered and looked menacingly at Audrey and Elleea. They proceeded to haul them off the train, which promptly left without them. 'Let us see your papers,' the soldiers ordered, assuming these two white people were mercenaries — an odd assumption to make as far as Audrey was concerned as women had never been in the mercenaries' ranks! Elleea replied in French, 'What are you doing?' (The soldiers' understanding of French was poor and Audrey was told later that they had confused the word 'mercenary' with the word 'missionary'.)

The Featherstones were due to board a banana boat late that evening ready to sail home the next day. The soldiers took them to a small hut and told them to wait. Two of the soldiers sat next to them and the two missionaries tried to make conversation. By this time, the soldiers had discovered that Audrey and Elleea were not mercenaries and were wondering what to do with them. After about three hours, a soldier opened the door and cried out, 'You can go on your way now. There will be a train in half an hour.'

A train arrived, but it was not a passenger train; it was one of the small trains that chugged from station to station so the

Congolese could go to market. It had no carriages and was full of chickens and goats. In their eagerness to get rid of Audrey and Elleea, the soldiers opened the train door and shoved them in, much to the astonishment of the people already on board. At the side of the compartment there was a narrow ledge, and as the two of them sat there, tired and bemused, the Congolese passengers 'examined them'.

Audrey and Elleea could not understand the language in that part of Congo, but the people were kind to them and someone gave them a banana. They had not eaten for hours. It gradually grew dark as the train rumbled on. When it stopped at an unknown destination, a fellow whispered to Elleea, 'Stay, stay.' The stranger left the compartment and within a few minutes returned with a candle for them. News of their presence had gone up and down the train, and a few Congolese came to greet them, asking, 'Are you missionaries?' They could not figure out why missionaries were on that particular train. Audrey managed to communicate that they were returning to England. Immediately their faces brightened, as they replied, 'Do you know what has happened in England? England have won the World Cup!'

Home at last!

They arrived at Matadi at midnight and left the train, not knowing what to do next. After what seemed like hours, someone from the Swedish mission approached them. 'We have been so worried! We were expecting you to arrive on the ordinary train. The boat has already left.' They were taken to a bungalow for a meal and a short nap, after which they managed to secure a passage on the *Mar del Plata*, which was leaving the next day. They checked with the purser's office about their cabin, expecting the usual one on the lower deck, but they were shown to 'more than a cabin' on the upper deck! They were given special treatment. After about half an hour into their journey, the boat stopped. The poor captain had been ordered to stop so the boat could be searched for mercenaries. 'Oh no!' thought the exhausted couple. Two hours later, they were on their way again, thankful that this time no one had searched their cases. Back in England, they were delighted to arrive at RBMU's headquarters at Balham.

20
A final term

Deputation work

When the Featherstones arrived home in the summer of 1966, they both went for medical check-ups and Elleea had the skin cancers on his face surgically removed. They travelled to Devon and stayed with Audrey's mother and her husband at Three Beaches between Brixham and Paignton for about ten days, before starting their deputation work.

In those days, missionary organizations, including RBMU, had regional secretaries all over the country, who were great supporters of the work and arranged meetings in their areas. So as soon as missionaries arrived home, they had a long list of engagements waiting to be fulfilled, some lasting a week or ten days. Audrey and Elleea attended numerous meetings all over Great Britain and Ireland, which they thoroughly enjoyed.

All change

At the end of the year, Audrey and Elleea received various letters from Congo, saying, 'We do hope you are coming back, even if it's only for two or three years!' It was a difficult decision for them both. It seemed to Audrey and Elleea as if the old ways and ethos of missionary work in Congo were disappearing. The new missionaries, with proper university qualifications to teach in French, were involved in secondary education and training Congolese to a much higher academic level. The Wrights were the only other experienced couple left and the Congolese were taking more responsibility for the spiritual well-being of the church. In other words, there was no obvious need for the Featherstones, who had spent all their time pastoring, preaching, teaching and evangelizing.

There was no doubt that Elleea had benefited from the furlough, and Audrey felt they should return to continue their work with the hundreds of villages deep in the forest, where tribal languages, not French, were spoken. Congo was still in a time of transition, however. The political situation was unstable, the infrastructure was damaged almost beyond repair, and many of the roads were impassable. For a young man, driving along dirt roads was a bearable necessity, but for Elleea, in fragile health, it was a genuine struggle. The hospitals were sparsely equipped with medical supplies and the schools had no pens or paper. There were no suitable Protestant universities in Leopoldville, which meant that many Congolese, having been through the new secondary schools, were moving to Europe, particularly Belgium, to continue their education.

New missionaries

When the Featherstones returned to Matadi early in 1967, they were accompanied by one of the new RBMU missionaries, an educationalist, who was heading for Baringa. His name was Simon Preswell* (*pseudonym). He was British and in his mid to late twenties. He was a pleasant enough young man, but both Audrey and Elleea got a bit of a shock when each night they heard him listening to the *Beatles* and other music groups on a new tape recorder! Audrey thought they must have appeared 'square and old fashioned' to him.

When Audrey had trained at Redcliffe in the 1940s and then moved to the mission field, she had known only too well that all the missionaries were senior to her; she was therefore extremely reticent to voice her opinion on any matter. Simon's attitude was completely different. He was much more laid back and was full of enthusiasm and ideas, which he freely expressed without any reservations or diffidence.

Between 1965 and 1967, nine or ten new young RBMU missionaries travelled to Congo. They were godly and Christlike in their attitudes and behaviour. As well as Simon, there was another young man called Matthew* and two girls, Lisa* and Rhiana*. Before long Simon was attracted to Rhiana and Matthew to Lisa. (Although Audrey had been engaged to Elleea before he went back to the field, RBMU did not allow them to marry until Audrey had been on the field and passed her first language exams.) Both couples disregarded protocol and headed off in one of the Land Rovers to Basankusu, found someone to officiate and got married! To them it seemed the sensible thing to do. They saw no reason why they should submit to a set way of doing things. Sadly, Matthew and Lisa were later both killed in a car accident.

RBMU, like other mission agencies, also experienced difficulties with incompatible personnel. An advisory group was set up to resolve difficulties. In extreme cases the person causing the conflict was either sent home or moved to another mission station. It was easier for married couples because they could live together, without interference, but for single missionaries, who had to share a house, there were times when personalities clashed, which was not a good testimony to give the Congolese.

Establishing the work

The Featherstones did not return to Baringa itself, but set up home in the *lifeta*. They still took meetings in the Lomongo language, and the majority of their time was spent teaching and evangelizing. Elleea was much better health-wise and preaching with authority and eloquence. The local pastors arranged conventions for preaching and teaching and Audrey took the Bible studies for the women.

They began to establish the work again, but with an entirely different emphasis. RBMU no longer had a dozen or so mission stations, each with a full complement of staff; instead, all their energies were expended on establishing a good Christian centre at Baringa (*lifeta*) for the training of church leaders, school teachers and young people to a much higher level of education — both secular and spiritual. There were big centres run by UFM, AIM and WEC more to the east and in Leopoldville (by this time renamed Kinshasa), but as yet nothing at Baringa.

Audrey with her ledgers at Baringa (1968)

As the old way of missionary work was dying out in Congo, Audrey and Elleea concentrated on preparing the up and coming generation, grounding them in the Word of God and putting godly spiritual Congolese leaders in place. With the maturing of the Congolese church, they both felt fairly sure that the Lord was leading them home for good, but after twenty-five years serving the people they loved, the prospect of never returning to Congo was hard to bear.

Goodbyes

In the weeks leading up to their final departure, the summer of 1969, Audrey and Elleea travelled to various villages, where the people crowded round them. The Congolese were sad at the thought of them leaving. They hugged them, prayed with them, and said, 'We shall all meet up in heaven!'

Their last Sunday in Congo was at Baringa, and the Congolese pastor there, David Bofaso, shared these verses with them: '*O bikole, londokoza, l'inyo banton lim'esi, lokwa! Yawe andetaki lim'aki'mi nda likunju; lim'aki'mi nda likunju ja ngoya aandaki lina likami. Ko aolila bomwa'okami boyale ng'ifaka y'etumba ya mpia, aondisa nda lililingi ja likata likdande, ko aondil'emi boala bondefwa, aompong'olotsi nda ntoto ekande*' (*Yesaya* 49:1-2). The translation is: 'Listen, O isles, unto me; and hearken, ye people, from far; the LORD hath called me from the womb; from the bowels of my mother hath he made mention of my name. And he hath made my mouth like a sharp sword; in the shadow of his hand hath he hid me, and made me a polished shaft [arrow]; in his quiver hath he hid me' (Isaiah 49:1-2).

They were presented with an arrow, the shaft of which was made out of wood from the boala tree. As the pastor handed over the arrow, he said, 'You are two of the Lord's arrows. Before you were born he called you and prepared you in every way to come to us. In his time, he put you in his bow and sent you to us here in Congo. When you came to bring the word of God to us, it was sharp like an arrow. You came and taught us. And now, after all these years, the Lord is putting you back

The Featherstones' final farewell. (Dr Arthur Wright is standing by the Land Rover's spare wheel.) Pastor David Bofaso is sending them off with a hymn, Bible reading and a prayer.

again into his bow and sending you back to your own country.'

Bofaso continued, 'The arrow belongs to the one who made it. It is his and he fashions it for his own use. When he shoots it, it will always fly straight to where he wants it to go. It does not turn off one way or the other, or turn back. When the Lord sent you here, you remained; you haven't gone back or turned to the left or the right. He made you like an arrow with a polished shaft — you were clean. The Lord Jesus kept you clean by his blood, so everything you did was straight. Through all the difficult times we have experienced together, the Lord always held us tightly in his hand and kept us safe in his quiver, close by his side.'

After emotional goodbyes, Audrey and Elleea travelled to the airstrip at Basankusu and caught the flight down to Kinshasa, where they stayed again at the United Missions Hostel. They had left all their household possessions for the new missionaries, so they were able to travel lightly, with their few remaining belongings in two suitcases. Their final journey back to the U.K. was uneventful.

Audrey looked back over her time as a missionary, and remembered God's faithfulness, goodness and love in so many different situations; the deep richness of his many blessings; and the godliness of colleagues and the Congolese pastors. She recalled how the presence of God had remained with them through the troubled times of independence and the Simba rebellion, and how in his mercy her Saviour had rescued Elleea from the storehouse fire. She thought about the times she had spent with those who had grown in their faith over the years and the sense of true fellowship and oneness she had been so privileged to enjoy. For such memories she gave thanks to God.

21
Adjusting to life in the UK

Family

On their arrival home, the Featherstones spent time with Elleea's three married brothers in the Cheltenham and Gloucester area, staying with Ken and his wife, who were hospitable and kind. They were churchgoers, who regarded themselves as good living people, but did not see any need of personal salvation. They were easy to talk to, outgoing and interested in missionary work. Both Audrey and Elleea had good opportunities to share Christ with them and to relate many of their experiences. Ken and his wife thought the work they had been doing in Congo was 'wonderful'.

Audrey's mother's husband had died some months previously and she was now living on her own at Three Beaches. They stayed with her for several months. She was finding widowhood a struggle and suggested that they move in with her on a permanent basis, but they declined her offer — a difficult decision but one they felt was right. Although they had little money, they needed to find a house of their own, even if it was small. Their desire was to open their home to young people and for Bible studies. Besides, they were still away for much of the time on deputation work. Without a car, Devon was not a convenient base from which to travel; they needed somewhere more central.

Buying a house

Elleea was eligible for a state pension and they also had a small pension from RBMU, which, taken together, were just about sufficient for their daily living. During their last term in Congo, knowing they were soon to return home, if anyone had sent them a monetary gift, they put it to one side ready for their retirement. In this way they had managed to save about £2,000, but it was nowhere near enough to buy a house!

They arranged to visit Audrey's sister, Pat, who lived in Milford-on-Sea (Hampshire), and travelled by coach to Bournemouth, where Pat met them. Pat was teaching at the Junior Church of England School in Milford-on-Sea so was busy for most of the day, but she encouraged them to make themselves at home, to relax and to enjoy walking in the area. She also asked, 'What are you going to do now? Where are you going to live? You must start looking for a property to buy. When you go to Lymington and the surrounding areas, go into the estate agents.'

Audrey and Elleea felt like a couple of school kids, without any knowledge of how to buy a house. The estate agents gave them details of the cheapest houses and they sat on a nearby bench and read through the information they had been given. All the flats, houses and bungalows for sale were at prices ranging from £6,000 - £20,000. There was nothing for £2,000.

Just before they visited Pat, they had received a letter from Arthur Tilsley to say that Arthur and Elizabeth Wright had written to tell him that they had received a small legacy, of which they had no need at that time as they were still out on the field. (The Wrights finally left Zaire in 1973.) They wanted to give Audrey and Elleea a loan from the legacy of £2,000 so they could find somewhere to live. 'We don't want this money sitting in the bank,' wrote Arthur. 'Give it to the Featherstones as from the Lord and tell them to repay it only when they are able.' When the Featherstones realized that even the smallest house was considerably more than £2000, they decided to take up the Wrights' kind offer. So they had £4000. Amazingly one estate agent gave them details of two houses priced at £5,000, so they decided to go and look at them — in faith! They particularly liked the one in New Milton, Hampshire.

When Audrey had first gone to Congo, she had known a girl called Cath, who stayed on the field for only one term; she returned home and married a godly Christian businessman named Victor. When Audrey and Elleea were home on furlough, they were often invited to stay with Cath and Victor in Swanage, Dorset. When Cath heard about their retirement she wrote and invited them to stay for a week, and she promised to arrange RBMU meetings in the vicinity at which they could speak.

So Audrey and Elleea went to Swanage and stayed with Victor and Cath, enjoying a happy time of fellowship as well as taking the meetings. Then one evening over supper, Cath asked them where they were going to settle. They told her they were praying about it and waiting for the Lord to guide them. Audrey mentioned that they had been house hunting. 'Did you see anything you liked?' asked Victor excitedly.

'Yes, we did see one we liked,' replied Audrey somewhat sheepishly, as she did not like to say much about the unaffordable price.

At the end of their stay, Cath took them to Bournemouth, where Victor worked. When they got into the car, Victor said, 'Now then, where is this house?'

'New Milton, but we can't go there — looking at it was just a bit of fun.' But no matter how much Audrey protested, Cath and Victor insisted on taking them to New Milton. When they arrived, they walked into the estate agents and one of the salesmen arranged to show them around; it was a newly built house with a garden but no garage. Audrey felt guilty because she knew they did not have enough money to buy it.

As they drove back to Bournemouth for a meal, Audrey and Elleea felt very confused. Then Victor said, 'You know, Cath and I feel that you should buy that house.'

'We're not sure about that,' chorused Audrey and Elleea.

Victor asked, 'How much money do you have?'

'About £4,000 in all.'

'Come along,' said Victor enthusiastically, and he took them to see Mr Bennett, a Christian solicitor. 'Even if you only have a small pension, you can get a small endowment mortgage.'

Audrey and Elleea looked at each other, 'What is an endowment mortgage?' With all sorts of questions running through their minds, they reluctantly entered Mr Bennett's office.

'I understand you need a bit of money to purchase a property,' said the elderly gentleman sitting behind his desk. He explained about the endowment mortgage and how to repay it — information that went in Audrey's one ear and out the other. 'I can arrange an endowment of £2,000.' Audrey immediately realized that with £6000 they would be able to buy the house in New Milton. 'Although your pension is very small,' continued Mr Bennett, 'you could pay back a little every month.'

Both Audrey and Elleea left the solicitors rather bewildered. Cath and Victor were waiting outside. Over a cup of tea, Victor said, 'You could get an endowment mortgage for £2,000, but you would have to pay interest. Instead Cath and I want to give you a loan of £2,000 without interest. You can repay it as and when you are able. Take it as from the Lord.'

Such a kind offer was impossible to resist, and they sensed it was the Lord's provision; so they duly went ahead and bought the property. Slowly but surely they accumulated furniture. Week by week they put a little aside. In this way within five or six years they were not only able to repay Victor's loan, but to repay Arthur and Elizabeth, who were returning to England and needed some money. They made new friends, and five or six people came regularly to the house for Bible studies.

Difficulty settling

Arthur Tilsley, a Brethren man, told everyone he could about the Featherstones' teaching gifts. At New Milton there was the Chelston Bible College, which met in a large house. About twenty to twenty-five young men and women, who wanted a deeper understanding of God's word, attended. Elleea was asked to give lectures there for some four to five years. Audrey also ended up taking numerous women's meetings.

They stayed in their house for two to three years, but found it difficult to settle in a church. The Baptist Church in New Milton was experiencing problems with their minister and the congregation was not happy. After a while they made friends with a couple who lived at Lymington and consequently they discovered that there was a new estate at Pennington where small bungalows were being built. The Baptist Church at Milford-on-Sea was also more Bible-based. So they sold their New Milton house and bought a bungalow at Pennington, which meant they were nearer Pat, Audrey's sister, and could regularly visit Audrey's mother, who had moved into the area.

By this time most of the Featherstones' deputation work had come to an end. Elleea continued to lecture at Chelston and Audrey enjoyed the women's meetings, but it was difficult to make ends meet. Audrey looked in the New Milton *Advertiser* and found a job cleaning for two mornings a week in a house owned by a rich couple; so for two years she hoovered, dusted and polished for a few extra pennies. The granddaughter of the couple often came to stay. She loved listening to Audrey as she told stories about the Congo mission field and the Lord Jesus Christ.

Lansdowne Baptist Church

While both Audrey and Elleea found life in England a real culture shock, what they missed most was the sound biblical teaching they had been used to in Congo. They made friends with a New Milton couple, Bill and Hazel Thwaites, who had recently moved into the area from Southampton. They often got together and enjoyed spiritual fellowship and a time of prayer. The Thwaites too could not find a church in which to settle.

In January 1976, Rev Harry Kilbride became minister of Lansdowne Baptist Church (LBC) in Bournemouth. Bill and Hazel had heard good reports of his preaching and asked their new friends if they would like to accompany them to LBC one Sunday. The four of them were richly blessed under Harry's ministry and started to attend regularly; but Audrey and Elleea were at a crossroads because, not being able to drive, they could only go to Lansdowne when Bill and Hazel took them. They prayed earnestly about whether Lansdowne was the right church for them, particularly as it would involve moving to Bournemouth, a town they did not like. After much agonizing in prayer, they decided to move and bought a flat in Wellington Road.

Bible studies

Miss Lily Rodaway, a rather austere 'Baptist' lady, was the secretary of the women's fellowship at Lansdowne, and at that time was responsible for booking speakers. She asked Audrey to speak on missionary work in Congo at one of the meetings, but on discovering that the date she had chosen fell on the church's *Day of Prayer*, she asked Audrey to speak on prayer instead, which was well received by those who attended.

During Harry Kilbride's time at Lansdowne, Margaret Detzler and June Kilbride ran a ladies' Bible study group, at the end of which was a time for questions and answers. After Harry and June left, and Margaret and her husband, Wayne, went to pastor Kensington Baptist Church in Bristol, it was hoped that the incoming minister's wife, Jill Buss, would take on the Bible studies. When she declined, Judith Berry, Eva Irvine and Mary Falkner-Lee, members at Lansdowne, having been so impressed with Audrey's teaching on prayer, all approached Audrey and asked her if she would consider leading the studies. Audrey, who was already taking occasional studies for a group of ladies from Christ Church, Westbourne, gave it much prayerful thought, as her 'style' had always been to teach rather than to lead a discussion group. Finally she agreed to lead the studies on a teaching basis for a trial period of three months — studies that continued for two years before Audrey stopped leading them to look after Elleea, whose health was rapidly deteriorating.

22
Elleea — to glory

From the beginning of their relationship, Elleea was a tower of strength for Audrey to lean on. He was a wise and experienced missionary who helped her to adjust to a new life in Congo and imparted to her his considerable knowledge. When times were hard, to bolster her faith, he often told Audrey about his two years of fulltime work with the Caravan Mission during the 1920s, and how he toured villages and farms in the West Country with a caravan. He lived by faith and his 'payment' was usually half a dozen eggs or some bacon!

Health problems

Audrey and Elleea had moved to Bournemouth in 1978, and for the first year Elleea was still lecturing at Chelston Bible College, but it soon became apparent that his health was deteriorating rapidly. Sometimes, when out walking, he suddenly stopped and started to shake violently all over. During these convulsions, which lasted about three or four minutes, he was unable to articulate properly. He visited the doctor and was diagnosed with diabetes.

After that, Elleea suffered one health problem after another, including a time in Christchurch Hospital with suspected prostate cancer. Audrey was still visiting her mother twice a week by train to help with gardening and shopping, but whenever she went, she was concerned for Elleea, as she never knew if he was going to be all right on his own.

Elleea then suffered his first stroke, which was a traumatic time for both of them. It was followed by smaller TIAs (transient ischaemic attacks). Their flat in Wellington Road was on the second floor and there was no lift, and Elleea was soon too frail to manage the stairs; so in 1985 they moved into a smaller flat with a lift, on the same road. When looking back to the early days of his illness, Audrey chided herself for not being as patient as she should have been with her husband.

Elleea was diagnosed with Parkinson's disease, a progressive neurological condition affecting movement. For about nine months the disease was accompanied with periods when he acted aggressively towards Audrey, a disconcerting time for her to say the least as it was so out of character for him to behave in that manner. Thankfully that phase passed, but he found it increasingly difficult to walk and needed a wheelchair whenever they went out. There were still good times, though. On one occasion, he thoroughly enjoyed a trip around Poole harbour in Bob and Judith Berry's boat, which reminded him of the many journeys he had taken by boat in Congo.

To glory

On 12 June 1987, the Featherstones celebrated their ruby wedding anniversary, which was a special occasion for them, but the days ahead were marked by a continued decline in Elleea's health. Various carers came in every day to help Audrey get him up in the morning and to put him to bed in the evening. Sometimes they came in twos to lift Elleea. If one started to swear, the other, remembering it was a Christian home, said, 'You don't say things like that here.' They liked visiting Elleea, remarking, 'Your home is different — there is a peace about it.'

Jane Cooper, a Christian friend, when she went round to help, saw Audrey's love and support for Elleea firsthand. She was amazed at how Audrey kept Elleea going; she encouraged him to walk a few steps using his zimmer frame and threw a ball to him, clapping like a child if he caught it. When he smiled, she showed great delight. 'Her whole life at this time,' said Jane, 'centred on giving her husband as rich a quality of life as possible. She was willing to put her life on hold to care for her husband in his time of great need.'

Judith Berry, who also witnessed Audrey's tender love and compassion, and unceasing and seemingly tireless patience with Elleea, which sometimes included the most demeaning duties, called her 'nothing but a perfect example of how to care for your nearest and dearest "in sickness and in health until death do us part"'.

Sheila Eaton, who visited Audrey and Elleea each week at this time to help them with the shopping, remarked, 'Two things that really impressed me as a young Christian were the peace, even joy, Audrey had despite her difficult situation; and her absolute devotion to Elleea. She was rarely deterred in her interactions with him, even when he became less responsive, and she worked hard to stimulate him. Once when I came back with the shopping, Audrey was rolling a football at Elleea's feet, trying to get him to kick the ball, in an attempt to keep him as physically active as possible. When he was hospitalized at Christchurch for about a week or two, Audrey found it so painful and difficult to be parted from him.'

For two years Audrey was unable to go to church, as all her time was taken caring for her husband — a sacrifice she did not mind at all. She was honoured to be able to nurse him at home. Finally, after a long brave fight, Elleea was called into the presence of his Saviour during the early hours of All Saints Day, 1 November 1991, at the age of eighty-eight. The struggle was at last over.

As she had promised to do, Audrey called Judith Berry and told her the sad news. Judith immediately drove to Audrey's flat and stayed with her until morning. Audrey did not contact any of her other friends during the night as she did not want to disturb their sleep.

Steve Brady, then pastor of Lansdowne, discussed the funeral arrangements with Audrey, who was concerned that as she had not been to church for such a long time no one would come to the thanksgiving service. In the end a good number attended, including many of Elleea's carers.

Life without Elleea

Not only did Audrey miss him terribly — 'her sense of loss was palpable' — but she had been so used to looking after him day and night, unable and unwilling to do anything else, that she did not know what to do with her spare time. She also dreaded going back to church. The thought of sitting among a crowd of people again was terrifying.

During this time, Judith Berry and her husband, Bob, were particularly kind and understanding. Two or three Sundays after Elleea died, they invited her to sit with them in the gallery during the morning service, after which they took her back to their home for lunch. This continued for the next two or three Sundays. Gradually Audrey adjusted. She soon got into the habit of walking to church on Sunday mornings unless it was raining.

Only a few weeks after her return, Mike and Gill Palmer asked her to speak on three consecutive Saturday evenings to the church *Network* group (late teens/early twenties) on the subject of prayer. Audrey did not feel any rapport with this age group, but agreed to go ahead. Between forty and fifty young people crammed into Bob and Ann Rule's home, which was a great encouragement to Audrey, who spoke from her heart over the three evenings. It was a perfect antidote for Audrey, as it helped her to think about other things.

Bible studies

A year or so after Elleea's death, Audrey moved out of the flat in Wellington Road that was filled with so many memories, to a flat in Boscombe, where she lives today. It was at about this time that her lunch time Bible studies resumed, which gave her the opportunity to share her knowledge of the Scriptures and Christian experience with other women.

Her grasp of the historical and geographical background to the books of the Bible made her studies come alive. Her sight was now deteriorating rapidly, which eventually meant she had to spend hours preparing for the studies by painstakingly moving a special magnifying glass across the page of a book, thus enlarging a tiny section of the text at a time. With a memory that was still sharp, she recalled dates and names, not only from the Bible, but from her reading of church history, which was a particular love of hers. She spoke for an hour, having learned her 'sermon' — she was unable to read her own notes. What she taught was both encouraging and challenging, and relevant to everyday life and Christian witness.

Her theology was reformed and she placed emphasis on repentance, the reverence and awe of God and the headship of Christ in his church. Her aim was to point to Christ and to exalt him, and to persuade others to know and love him in an ever-deepening way. She was not a fan of the 'modern' evangelism that makes salvation dependent on a person's decision, rather than on Christ. In speaking on the 'perseverance of the saints', she said, 'Yes, *but* only he who endures to the end will be saved. The important thing to know is whether or not you are truly born again. Decisions and praying the "sinner's prayer" are not enough; there must be a genuine work of the Holy Spirit bringing new birth.'

It was through preparing these Bible studies for the benefit of others that she began to overcome the grief of losing such a dearly loved husband. Life for Audrey was never the same again after Elleea's death, but she learned to cope, and her strong Christian faith turned her heart heavenwards to the one whose love never fails. 'Now unto him that is able to keep you from falling, and to present you faultless before the presence of his glory with exceeding joy, to the only wise God our Saviour, be glory and majesty, dominion and power, both now and for ever. Amen' (Jude 24-25).

Appendix 1
A history of RBMU

Regions Beyond Missionary Union (RBMU) was born, along with other agencies, as a result of the evangelical revival that took place during 1858–1859 — a revival that awakened the churches in America and Britain to the Bible's authority in all matters of faith and practice, and to the importance of prayer. Henry Grattan Guinness, RBMU's founder and one of the heralds of the revival, said, 'The Spirit of revival that broke out in Britain and America had taken hold of me. I was prepared for it though I knew it not, but only yearned to be a burning and shining light for God among men.'

Henry Grattan Guinness

In 1866 Henry Grattan Guinness, a nephew of Arthur Guinness, the founder of the famous brewing empire, invited James Hudson Taylor of the China Inland Mission (CIM) to his apologetics class in Dublin. Guinness hoped that the famous missionary might set ablaze the hearts of his students for world evangelization.

When Taylor appealed for missionaries to go to China, ten out of the twelve students volunteered, including Guinness, but Taylor encouraged his new friend to stay at home and train the men and women converted in the revival, whose lack of education barred them from the larger denominational missions. 'If you train them, CIM will accept them,' promised Taylor, whose work with CIM inspired Grattan to serve the unreached interior populations of the great continents, which led in 1878 to the

Henry Grattan Guinness

birth of the Livingstone Inland Mission (LIM) to Central Africa, precursor of RBMU.

Taylor's suggestion about training converts prompted Guinness, with his wife Fanny, to establish the East London Training Institute for Home and Foreign Missions in Stepney Green (1873), across the road from the Mission Hall of his friend Thomas Barnardo and around the corner from the East London Tabernacle, which had a seating capacity of 2,000 and a Sunday school of hundreds of children.

By then Guinness, later described as an 'Irish revivalist, catalyst of world evangelisation, noted astronomer, and a prolific author of commentaries on Biblical prophecy', was already a preacher of note, attracting crowds of up to 10,000 at a time. Elizabeth Pritchard says, 'He was welcome everywhere. All over the British Isles people flocked in their thousands to hear the handsome young preacher with the eloquent tongue and golden voice. The results of these meetings were fantastic, for God was with him as he pleaded with men to repent and believe the gospel.'

Even *The Daily Express* mentioned his success: 'Mr Guinness preached yesterday in York Street Chapel. The attendance was greater than on any former occasion. In the evening it amounted to 1,600, and if there were a place large enough, five times that number would have been present to hear this highly gifted preacher ... The interest he has excited has daily increased and probably will continue to do so during his labours in Dublin.' Edwin Orr classed Guinness as one of the great preachers of the nineteenth century along with D. L. Moody and Charles Spurgeon.

The East London Institute (ELI)

The first student of the college, Joshua Chowriappah, an Asian man from India, enrolled at the beginning of 1873. He spoke so little English that the Guinnesses decided he should live with them at Clapton. By the end of that year the college had moved two miles east to Harley House, a large old-fashioned property with a delightful garden. Harley House in Bow became the mission headquarters for generations to come. Later expansion

THE EAST LONDON INSTITUTE

For Home and Foreign Missions.

Harley House and College, and Doric Lodge, Bow, London, E.;

AND

Hulme Cliff College, Curbar, Derbyshire.

Hon. Director—H. Grattan Guinness, D.D., F.R.G.S.

Hon. London Director—H. Grattan Guinness, Jun., M.R.C.S., F.R.G.S.

This Institute was founded in March, 1872, with a view to increase the number of ambassadors for Christ among the heathen, and in the darker regions of Christendom.

The East London Institute

included a large country mansion and estate in Derbyshire (Cliff College 1875), which became a training centre for workers going to Congo, and a separate college for women (Doric Lodge 1884), which provided an equally diversified curriculum, with the addition of midwifery training. In 1889, the Lodge expanded to Bromley Hall, an old mansion.

From the outset, the Institute offered students a mixture of theory combined with opportunities for practical work with Thomas Barnardo in the slum areas of the East End. Principal Forbes Jackson, later described the East End training ground: 'Here are souls as indifferent as can be found on any pagan soil; slums whose squalor would reek even in China. Crowds who fill these busy streets afford fine opportunity for the callow youths who will later stand up in mela or bazaar. He who keeps his heart up in the East End of London, will keep hopeful even in Congo.' Guinness too was convinced that anyone who could not cope with life among London's poorest, would be unlikely to survive the rigours of Congo.

No tuition fees were charged and no salaries offered, as the Institute was to be run by faith alone, and no suitable volunteers were refused. Mission halls were opened throughout East London for meetings and teaching, and soon the students were preaching to 12,000 people weekly. The Institute purchased its own mission yacht, the 'Evangelist', to ferry students and their message to seamen on their ships. Harley College, a new two-storey facility, opened in 1878. George Adams, a Harley student, wrote, 'These are the foundations upon which Harley College was built — faith in God's word, faith in the power of prayer, faith in the presence of God, joyful obedience to his commands.' A nursing centre and medical mission, and a publishing division were formed later.

The Institute was both interdenominational and international, with twenty nationalities represented in the student body, and committed to sending its workers to the poor regions peripheral to and beyond the British Empire — literally reaching the parts other missionary organizations found difficult to reach. By 1903, some 887 men and 281 women had been trained for missionary service all over the world, with a wide

Harley College, Bow

variety of missionary organizations. Of these, 215 left to work in Africa, 182 in Asia, 170 in the Americas and twenty-six in Australia. Twelve years later, 1,500 young missionaries had been sent around the world, representing thirty different denominations in forty mission agencies.

Congo

With the death of David Livingstone in May 1873, coupled with Henry Morton Stanley's reports to the *New York Herald*, and his book *Through the Dark Continent*, thrusting the barbarities of the slave traffic onto the evangelical conscience, interest in Africa reached an all time high. In 1878, after 'fervent prayer for the millions of dark souls who had never heard the name of Jesus', and with the adopted name The Livingstone Inland Mission, the Guinnesses and a group of friends arranged for the first party of Harley College missionaries to travel to Congo, a largely unknown region, annexed as the private estate of King Leopold II of Belgium. Led by Strom, a Danish sailor, and Henry Craven of Liverpool, they followed the track opened by Stanley along the cataract region of lower Congo.

Craven only lived for seven years, but he managed to develop a Congo-English, English-Congo dictionary with a list of useful sentences for missionaries and travellers. In his last report to Harley House, he wrote, 'Although I cannot report any conversions, yet both Mr Harvey [Charles Harvey was soon invalided home] and myself are of the opinion that at three of our stations a crisis is at hand, when some will come out boldly for Christ.' He was right.

'The first Pentecost on the Congo'

Revival reached lower Congo in 1884 and by 1887 over a thousand converts had been added to the churches. In 1889 alone, some 950 were baptized and the Banza Manteka church numbered 1,500 members, many of whom evangelized the surrounding villages. One visitor exclaimed, 'The poison-giving, the throat cutting, the demoniacal yells, the diabolical dance

Map of Congo

and witchcraft are things of the past here. "Old things have passed away, and behold, all things are become new."'

Banza Manteka, the third LIM station, became the first Christian parish, with 2,000 being baptized. By the end of the century, Banza Manteka missionaries had nearly 3,000 pupils in sixty schools, and hundreds were being baptized each year. Other stations experienced similar awakenings, which continued after Grattan Guinness transferred the field to the American Baptists Missionary Union (ABMU). One station report commented, 'We are in the midst of a revival that equals the Banza Manteka Pentecost in intensity and surpasses it in extent.'

At the time the LIM was handed over to the ABMU, a transfer that was like the 'amputation of a limb' to Harry Guinness, there were seven operational bases, all on the south side of the Congo River, extending along 700 miles, with twenty-four missionaries in place. Many missionaries were happy to continue their work in Congo under the Americans, but John McKittrick, an 'immensely likeable Irishman' from Belfast and one of the original lower Congo party, was frustrated at their policy of consolidation. He wanted to extend their lines to upper Congo, so just before his furlough he obtained permission to explore by canoe the Balolo (iron people) territory, an adventure that marked 'the beginning of a century of ministry in Congo's heartland'.

Congo Balolo Mission (CBM)

McKittrick returned to Harley House with a burden for Baloloand, a vast unevangelized area with an estimated ten million inhabitants, lying south of the great horseshoe bend of the Congo River. He wanted LIM to re-enter Congo, and the American Baptists were happy to release him for his new venture, which was named Congo Balolo Mission. It adopted for its sphere the six southern tributaries of the Congo beyond Equatorville.

McKittrick travelled back to Congo in 1889 with seven new recruits and a vision for the peoples above the Stanley Pool. They trekked the 230 miles of unnavigable rapids, arriving at Bonginda, village of the most important chief on the river. It was here among the Ngombe tribe that RBMU's abiding legacy

The first Christian church in Congo

was left in Congo with thousands of converts and hundreds of churches established.

During the thirteen years from 1889 through 1902, twenty-nine out of thirty-five missionaries died, twelve laying down their lives in their first year, and twelve in their second and third years of service. Only six of the thirty-five lived on into the new century. Gustav Haupt, whose grave lies next to John McKittrick's, wrote of his fallen comrades, 'They are buried stones for the future building of God.' The students at Harley College, who seemed more determined than ever to pour into Africa in a 'suicidal stream', referred to Congo as 'The Shortcut to Heaven', and one missionary wrote home, 'Africa kills all her lovers.'

In 1908 the challenge to evangelize Upper Congo was still as real as ever. Harry Guinness wrote in that year: 'Missionary effort has only touched the fringe of Upper Congo's need ... We have only been permitted to occupy a comparatively restricted area.'

Edward Algernon Ruskin

One Congo pioneer who was particularly fruitful was Edward Ruskin, a former Harley College and Cliff College student, and a gifted linguist. Before long he was fluent in the Lomongo language and had defined the grammar. His determination to develop a vocabulary and to find the right turn of phrase earned him two nicknames: 'The one who pesters us with questions', and 'he who carries the little book to write words.'

By 1908 he had printed the Lomongo New Testament and in 1930 he had the 'supreme joy of seeing the whole Bible printed in the Lomongo language'. Two years earlier he had published a huge dictionary, which was soon followed by the *Grammar* and then *Notes on the Lingombe Grammar*. In addition, he produced many schoolbooks. So great was his output that Edward and his wife, Lily, a faithful helper, were honoured by Leopold, the Belgian king. One of Ruskin's last official acts in Congo was in 1938 to preside over the opening of the Mompono Bible Institute, which had an assembly hall, four

John McKittrick

classrooms and a first class of thirteen students representing four mission stations and three different tribal groups.

The pioneering work of men like McKittrick and Ruskin was foundational to establishing the work of Christ in Congo. So much so that by 1916 forty-two missionaries were serving in nine stations covering an area the size of England and four decades later 'there were 32,000 members on the church rolls, 9,000 children in schools, nineteen pastors, and eighty-eight evangelists'. A hospital was opened at Baringa in 1932, another at Yoseki in 1945, and three years after that a hospital was built at Yuli.

Expansion

To encourage support, the Regions Beyond Helpers Union was formed in 1892 and membership reached 11,000 by 1897, in which year the Institute took responsibility for the support of Harley students working in Peru and later for others in Argentina. In 1899 the Bihar and Orissa Mission to India commenced. The following year the Institute was renamed Regions Beyond Missionary Union, not simply in recognition of its growing global outreach, but because of the name of its magazine *Regions Beyond*, the American influence (missionary union is the American synonym for missionary society), and Paul's pioneering missionary hope expressed in 2 Corinthians 10:16: 'To preach the gospel in the regions beyond you, and not to boast in another man's line of things made ready to our hand.' RBMU was formally incorporated in 1903. Five years later RBMU had ninety-one missionaries — twenty-two in Argentina, sixteen in Peru, forty-two in Congo, and eleven in India.

Throughout the twentieth century the magazine *Regions Beyond* (from 1981 *Horizons*) published news of the mission's work. Conferences were organized, and pamphlets, books, lantern-slides, photographs and films were produced to raise awareness and increase support.

Henry Grattan Guinness died in 1910. Joseph Adams, a former Guinness student, spoke for multitudes when he noted, 'We all felt that the church of Christ militant had lost one of its great missionary leaders.' Five years later his son, Harry

Guinness, died at age fifty-three. Both deaths deprived the mission of vital leadership. Financial difficulties were acute during World War I, which curtailed development, and while the mission continued to operate in Congo and India, the South American work passed to the Evangelical Union of South America.

The period after World War II was, however, a time of expansion with the Peru Inland Mission coming under RBMU's umbrella in 1948. Borneo (Kalimantan Barat), and Dutch New Guinea (Irian Jaya) soon became RBMU's largest fields of work, both in terms of the number of missionaries and the dramatic growth of the church. From its base in northern India, RBMU became the main strength of the United Mission to Nepal, a coalition of mission agencies, which helped the tiny Nepal church to grow from twenty-five baptized believers in 1960 to its present size of over 50,000.

In more recent times, RBMU entered the Philippines, where the work quickly grew. Within fourteen years, thirty-five missionaries were witnessing for Christ in six major areas on the islands. Chile, in South America, also became a centre for RBMU's church planting policy, while the West African country of Cameroon was transformed into a centre for translation work, evangelism and leadership training courses among six distinct people groups.

Division

Almost inevitably, in spite of its many successes, some began to question the role and purpose of the mission, especially in relation to the indigenous churches and other organizations. The wide diversity of fields stretched resources and administration, and the idea of cooperating with other similar agencies was increasingly proposed. The North American councils, which had met as separate bodies since 1948, sometimes took a different view on important issues, and in 1979 the London based RBMU split from its overseas councils, the latter operating as RBMU International.

In the UK the mission became more involved in joint projects and in 1980 moved to office premises shared by other agencies. It still sought ways to maintain its own identity and considered expanding into new areas such as Pakistan and Thailand. However, from the late 1980s it became increasingly clear that it was no longer viable for the mission to continue as it was. In 1990, after negotiations with other bodies, the work in each area passed to new or existing agencies, although some missionaries remained with RBMU until 1991. In 1995 RBMU International merged with World Team, a global missionary fellowship formed in 1928 by Elmer Thompson and B. G. Lavastida as a small Bible Institute in central Cuba.

Appendix 2
'Yenzele — the Fetish Man'

Although the following true story is somewhat verbose and flowery in its language, it portrays a vivid picture of everyday life in Congo and the struggles and dangers missionaries faced. It was first published by RBMU in about 1962.

CONGO BUSH STORIES: 'Yenzele — the Fetish Man'
by Audrey Featherstone

Dingdong ding! Dingdong ding! Dingdong ding!

The little Congo urchin perched high on the anthill pulled in an abandoned ecstasy of childish delight at the long frayed rope attached to the rusty old bell swinging furiously above his woolly head.

Dingdong ding! Dingdong ding! Clang! Clang! Clang! Come to prayer! Come! Come!

The harsh, compelling notes spilled out into the mission compound, into the village and forest beyond, into the breathless, intense heat of the middle afternoon: a curious impact of sharp resonant sound striking against a solid barrier of humidity and heat.

Away up in the tiny leaf-roof covering of the bell-house a swarm of hornets flew madly to and fro, wildly desperate in this sudden cataclysm of sound and vibration as they sought desperately to escape its torments.

A long, slender snake, vividly green, lying coiled in the lazy warmth of the thick, tousled grass at the foot of the bell house, slithered with incredible swiftness towards the deep, dark shelter of its jungle home.

Dingdong ding! Dingding, dong!

In Class V, the missionary Mama, uncomfortably conscious of the steady trickles of perspiration trickling down her back and legs, paused in the middle of her French lesson to glance instinctively at the clock on the wall. Four o'clock — another half hour to go. She sighed imperceptibly with relief. The boys, unused to long periods of study and concentration, were becoming sleepy and unresponsive in the sultry closeness of the afternoon. Their clumsy, unmanageable, adolescent legs sprawled in all directions. Shirts sticky with sweat, hung limply to strong, young shoulders drooping in weariness against the desk behind. Eyes and minds, heavy with drowsiness, struggled half-heartedly with the grammar exercise before them. '*Le pronom relative est...*'

Ding dong ding! Ding dong ding!

The missionary nurse glanced with surprise at her watch. That time already! The long line of outpatients, gathered since 2:00 p.m. for their 'needles' in a continual hubbub of noise and altercation, had slowly diminished as the hot afternoon wore on. Now just two remained, sitting quietly and patiently in the shade of the massive breadfruit tree. Along the sun-drenched walk, now practically deserted, an African nurse passed quickly, surreptitiously loosening the ties of his apron as he went. Just another two ... Methodically and carefully she took up her syringe...

Dingdong ding! Dingdong ding! Ding ding!

Over the tops of the mission wooden bungalows, silent and lifeless under the brilliant blue sky, it sounded. It sounded over the top of the schoolhouse, over the top of the dispensary, over the top of the maternity block where soft brown, pink-palmed, gorgeous Congo babies slept soundly for the while in their little white cribs. It sounded over the tops of the workers' houses and cookhouses away out to the village where children played in the shade of the palms, shouting and laughing, teasing and quarrelling; where women pounded and kneaded in their airless, dark, smoke-filled cook-houses, working silently and mechanically, interrupting the steady rhythm of their labours only occasionally as they poured harsh torrents of scolding onto some disobedient child or, perhaps, let out a virulent stream of abuse upon the hapless head of an unloved neighbour; where old men sat lazily, indolent in the sombre stuffiness of their rude mud huts.

Ding-dong-ding-dong-ding-dong-ding-dong-ding!

In a final frenzied burst of ringing, the small boy released his hold on the rope and flew madly, exultantly down the steep side of the anthill, leaving the cord swinging drunkenly to and fro in the brilliant sunshine. The sound stopped abruptly and sharply, and in the sudden welcome silence the low, persistent hum of scattered human voices rose and fell in a pleasant undulation of sound.

Alone in his tiny office the missionary pondered over his message for the Bible study and prayer meeting due to take place that evening at 4:45 p.m. '*Ele Nzakomba ntatokaaka bolimo w'ofolu lolo bolimo wa mpamba.*' 'Not the spirit of fear but of power, of love, of a sound mind.' 'Not the spirit of fear, but of POWER.' 'Dear Lord, even this.' In an agony of pleading he bowed his head, 'and deliver them who through fear of death were all their lifetime subject to bondage'. The sun sank lower in the western sky, casting longer shadows across the ground still shimmering in the burning heat of late afternoon.

In a moment of time the lazy calm lay shattered in a thousand fragments as girls and boys released at last from the confines of the school, pushed and jostled their way out of the classrooms. Running and skipping, tumbling and falling in a perfect tumult of noise they scattered in all directions. To the dormitory, to the bureau, to the village, to the football field, to the forest, to the river, anywhere and everywhere, leaving behind them on the once tidy, clean mission paths, a trail of torn-up scraps of paper, half-sucked oranges, whittlings of wood, and — that thorn in the flesh of all missionaries — the white, dry spat out fragments of sugar cane.

The station drums beaten furiously by four long-legged young drummers sent out their deep, throbbing, intricate pattern of sound to the world around. The noise was both exhilarating and stimulating — Congo on the move, Congo alive, Congo with something to say. The drumming ceased as abruptly as it began and gradually the cheerful, uninhibited shouts and laughter of these dark-skinned children faded away as the last small groups wandered off to enjoy their few, brief hours of play and freedom. Down the sandy path leading to the church the older folk, in one's and two's, unhurriedly and quietly made their way.

The missionary standing before his tiny congregation felt unaccountably depressed. Somewhere, somehow, there was something wrong. A consciousness of near evil, a strange premonition of 'spiritual wickedness', would not be shaken off. The station folk, mostly men, had come to the meeting in desultory enough fashion, slumping heavily on the hard wooden benches as though tired and dispirited. Of the village people there was scarcely a sign. Something was wrong, somewhere, but what? He shivered, suddenly cold, and then pulling himself together proceeded with the meeting. 'For God hath not given us a spirit of fear but of power and...' He hesitated in his reading and caught his breath sharply. The scattered congregation sat up in an instant, alert and watchful. From the direction of the village a deep, mighty roar of frenzied human voices smote the air again and again. The noise was sinister and unnerving, gaining every second in momentum and volume as they sat there listening.

'For God hath not given us a spirit of fear but of power.' The little company started as the quiet, firm voice cut across the hundred and one fears and dreads that so unexpectedly had invaded their hearts and minds. '*Boikyi'okiso Yesu, ondimolaki iwa* — who has abolished death.' The words for a moment held and strengthened them, stilling their fears but not for long. A renewed spate of roaring and shrieking brought again to the surface the dark, superstitious pagan beliefs of endless ages. Restlessly they sat the meeting out, present in their bodies but emotionally a thousand dark years of satanic bondage away.

Out in the village, standing before the doorway of a tiny mud hut was a man. Round his neck, on a filthy piece of string, hung an outsize medal. In his hand he held an empty beer bottle, a withered bunch of croton leaves stuck down its neck. In his other hand he clutched a large white handkerchief. His bleary bloodshot eyes stared intently beyond the doorway into the miserable drabness of the room beyond, whilst beads of perspiration rolled down his face and neck. Behind him, completely blocking the village path, stood the village people, pulsating with excitement, amazement and fear, their faces, too, damp and sticky.

In the doorway, a woman crouched, trembling violently as with ague. Sick with apprehension her eyes followed the movements of the man before her who, with deliberate steps, crossed the threshold of her hut. Breathlessly the people watched, hands over mouths in an agony of suspense. He stood for a moment, motionless and then with a quick decisive movement set the beer bottle with its decoration of faded croton leaves on the floor of the hut. Taking the handkerchief he held it at arm's length, for perhaps half a minute, and then, in one complete, twirling, theatrical gesture, let that too fall to the ground.

Somewhere outside a baby goat bleated plaintively and piteously for its mother, the only sound to break upon this satanic drama being played out in all its mockery and cruelty.

The man, arms now folded, remained perfectly still but his tilted chin and lower lip protruding unmistakably in the direction of a smoke-blackened basket, spoke volumes. The woman neither spoke nor moved. A fluttering impatient sigh swept through the crowd stilled instantly as, with another rapid jerk, the thick lip again indicated the basket. With a little moan she moved across to the basket and reluctantly, hopelessly, removed its pathetic contents: a packet of yoko, a plantain, an old water pot, a handful of palm nuts, a few sticks and leaves. She paused, unhappily aware of the remorseless figure standing behind her, and then slowly, slowly her toil-worn hand reached down for the last wee packet and set that too on the ground. The man watching nodded faintly and with an odd, cunning little smile gathered up the bottle, the handkerchief and the packet, then stepped out triumphantly into the sunshine.

Pandemonium broke loose. The crowd reacted as though it were possessed, shrieking, yelling and screaming in a paroxysm of fearful amazement and guilty relief.

'The fetish is found, the fetish is found. He has discovered her fetish with his mighty magic. He is Wonder itself. Let us kill her, let us kill her!' Like a crowd of dervishes they exulted, bending and twisting their bodies into contortions both suggestive and menacing.

The woman cowed in her hut in an agony of fear and complete desolation. Her charm was gone, her sole protection against all the malignancy of evil that sought day by day to destroy her, was there no longer. With one poignant ear-splitting wail she threw herself to the ground and rocked violently to and fro in the filth of the mud floor.

The crowd, no longer concerned, turned off down the street shouting and screaming still. They followed their leader like so many puppets, intoxicated and fevered by the displays of magical power he had exhibited before their very eyes; the exposure of another man's miserable fetish a vicarious sop to their own guilt-ridden consciousnesses. Reaching another hut the man stopped again, the people following him jostling expectantly. Unseen and unnoticed a dark figure slipped furtively from the back of the hut and, slipping into the lengthening evening shadows, disappeared like a ghost into the forest. The crowd and the man waited, uncomprehending, before the silent, deserted house.

This was Yenzele, the fetish man; the man with a fetish more potent than all fetishes; the man sent by a local chief to travel throughout all the villages to discover and bring to light by the great magical properties of his fetish, all the charms and bad medicine belonging to the people. There had been several men, magicians, going round in recent years but no one so clever and powerful as Yenzele. The chief, nominally, was a Christian. Was he not a baptized Roman Catholic and did he not wear a large medal round his neck as a sure sign of his new-found religion? But he was also afraid. He had his medal and he had also his own collection of charms and fetishes purchased in times past from the witchdoctor. But he was still afraid. Why were people dying? Why were not more babies born? Why was the population of his area diminishing? Were there not *baloki* everywhere, sorcerers able to cause death and untold calamity with their special charms and fetishes hidden away in their death pots and other strange places? But Yenzele — he would surely find them out. He was afraid, desperately afraid. What *baloki* might at this very time be set against even him?

Yenzele! Yenzele! Yenzele!

Far into the night the insistent, monotonous, throbbing beat of the dance drums carried on in the close night air. Sweating figures stamped and capered, postured and gesticulated, their writhing shadows grotesque in the beautiful mosaic of light and shade formed by the radiantly silver moonbeams reaching down through the long, fairy-like fingers of the tall, dew-drenched palms.

Yenzele! Yenzele! Yenzele!

The strong, heady fumes of native palm wine and European beer coursed through their veins like burning fire as the drummers, their long dark wrists and fingers moving with incredible speed and delicacy of touch, urged the explosive rhythm faster and yet faster. The missionaries tossed and turned sleeplessly on their beds in the darkness of the warm, sultry night. 'Say among the heathen that the LORD reigneth.' 'Not of fear but of power, of love and of a sound mind.' 'Oh Lord Jesus, how long?'

Yenzele! Yenzele! Yenzele!

The children in the dormitories, two by two on the hard wooden beds, slept fitfully, dreams and nightmares chasing their subconscious minds, causing them to start and cry out in their sleep in pain and fear. A small boy awoke suddenly with a scream of terror. '*Al' endo, al' endo, ekeli emi endo!*' 'A dwarf is here, standing by me!' The children, startled awake, took up the cry '*A bokaji* [evil spirit] *is come, a bokaji is come!*' The missionary, slipping softly from his bed, ran swiftly across to comfort the children.

The missionary awoke with a start and looked at his watch. 4:45 a.m. — another day. It was yet dark and still as still, not a sound save that of the crickets chirping shrilly and incessantly.

He dressed quietly and came outside, catching his breath at the sheer, unutterable loveliness of that early, early morning. The tiny mission clearing set as a pool in the midst of the thick, tropical forest lay silver shining and clean in the soft, clear moonlight. The stars above twinkled and shone in a cloudless sky of deepest velvet. With a deep sigh of peace and joy he turned to his tiny office and took his Bible.

By noon the sun was riding high, a ball of molten fire in a burning sky. Soon the afternoon's work began; first the usual two o'clock clamour and then the low, steady hum of subdued activity. Suddenly an unexpected cry and roar of a huge unrestrained mob pouring on to the mission compound brought immediate confusion and disruption. The crowd shuffled to a stop, excited and curious as Yenzele stepped forward, his blood shot eyes uncertain for a moment as the missionary approached.

'*Nsoya wae...*' His words trailed off limply and nervously. 'You have come, yes,' the words shot out quickly and angrily. 'You have come like a madman bringing this crowd on your heels, without permission, without greeting, without politeness, turning our compound into an uproar. Now you will go, taking all these people with you. If you have anything to say to me, you will come alone and sober!' He paused, 'Now go, every single one of you.'

Shamefacedly and awkwardly they turned about. Yenzele half paused, chagrined and discomfited, but changing his mind walked insolently down the path. The missionary sighed, his mind full of strange foreboding. Why had they come? What did they know? What evil thing would there be here to be revealed by one whose coming was 'after the workings of Satan, with all powers and signs and lying wonders?' 'Not the spirit of fear.'

'*Bondele, nsoy.*' Yenzele stood on the veranda steps quietly, clean and sober and polite. It was seven o'clock, the time of the evening meal; the village streets and station paths were practically deserted. The '*bondele*', surprised, came out and returned his greeting. 'Well,' he said, 'and what is it?' '*Bondele*, I'm sorry about this afternoon, truly I fell in that palaver. But it is this — there is a fetish hidden away in your station church;

it has been kept there for years.' The missionary recoiled as though struck with a whip. In the church! In the house of God! A fetish, a revolting, dirty heathen fetish! Never! It could not be!

It WAS there. Hidden away in a secret cavity underneath the doorway of the church. It had been there for years, used and worshipped by its owner throughout that time. The people had known of its presence though not its whereabouts. They had suspected its owner but fear had sealed their lips. In the presence of magic and witchcraft all but the very finest 'of the wheat' lose their moral courage and integrity and remain passive and negative through fear of reprisal. They may not acquiesce, but neither will they protest against the use of and belief in, witchcraft. 'A smoking flax he shall not quench.' Oh, for those 'strong in the Lord and in the power of his might' in this mighty land of Africa.

The man who owned it was a church member. Week by week he had stood and prayed for the salvation of his heathen neighbours! He had even asked to be allowed to preach, but, thank the Lord, the missionaries had never felt led to let him do so. Now, here was one of his fetishes, his most important one; others were found later. A powerful fetish with a powerful curse — or so they believed, a fetish able to bring to nought all his enemies and rivals and prosperous neighbours and to bring to himself and his family alone, riches, children, prosperity, position and power. A fetish placed in the sanctuary of God for safekeeping and stronger influence. 'They worship me with their lips but their hearts are far from me.' An agony of failure and shame filled the missionary's heart. What a reproach to the peerless name of Christ! Who WAS sufficient for these things?

Yenzele! Yenzele!

This is modern Africa, the Africa of today not a hundred years ago; an Africa of seething unrest, of high ambition and aspiration; an Africa of fear and hopelessness, of dread and desolation, of cunning and cruelty and deep seated superstitions; a dark people living still in a dark world. We build our schools. We build our hospitals. We build our churches. What of the foundations? God grant that the foundations may ever be none other than JESUS CHRIST, crucified, risen and glorified. God grant that the builders, his chosen builders, may not refuse his call.

A wide range of Christian books is available from Evangelical Press. If you would like a free catalogue please write to us or contact us by e-mail. Alternatively, you can view the whole catalogue online at our website: www.evangelicalpress.org.

Evangelical Press
Faverdale North, Darlington, Co. Durham, DL3 0PH, England
e-mail: sales@evangelicalpress.org

Evangelical Press U.S.A.
P. O. Box 825, Webster, New York 14580, USA
e-mail: usa.sales@evangelicalpress.org

COMING SOON

The Life of Rowland Hill:
'The second Whitefield'

Author: Tim Shenton

Evangelical Press

ISBN-13: 978 0 85234 631 0

From the Foreword
'Here is biography at its best. Shenton marvellously brings Rowland Hill to life in a balanced and objective way, neither minimizing his remarkable set of gifts nor hiding his destructive blemishes ... You will find no dull pages in this book.'

***Dr Joel R. Beeke**, President and Professor of Systematic Theology and Homiletics, Puritan Reformed Theological Seminary, Grand Rapids, Michigan*

'This new book by Tim Shenton is a delight. We are given an excellent portrayal of Rowland Hill, the man, his times and his achievements under God, as well as fresh incentive for praise to God and prayer that he might raise up like men in our day of small things.'

***Dr Michael A. G. Haykin**, Principal and Professor of Church History and Reformed Spirituality, Toronto Baptist Seminary, Toronto*

'An exceptional biography — a ***must*** for the library of every serious Christian.'

***Brian H. Edwards**, Christian author, lecturer and teacher*

'An Iron Pillar': The Life and Times of William Romaine

Author: Tim Shenton

Evangelical Press

ISBN-13: 978 0 85234 562 7

William Romaine is a much neglected figure of eighteenth-century Evangelicalism. This book is the first modern biography of a complex and often bittersweet character. Drawing from original and often little-known sources, Tim Shenton provides a clear, consistent, and remarkably fair portrait of Romaine and the times in which he lived.

From Romaine's early years as a student of Oxford University, to his appointment as a rector in the Church of England, to his profoundly influential ministry in London, to his numerous inspiring relationships (with such figures as John and Charles Wesley, George Whitefield, Lady Huntingdon and Henry Venn), to his final post at Blackfriars, the author guides the reader to a deeper understanding of the eighteenth-century evangelical scene.

'This volume deserves to be read by as many as possible. Ministers should read it because it describes a servant who was devoted to the calling of his Master and whose service was owned by his Master. Those interested in church history will discover fresh insights into a crucial period of British church life. Believers should read it in order to be stimulated to pray for revival.'

The Monthly Record

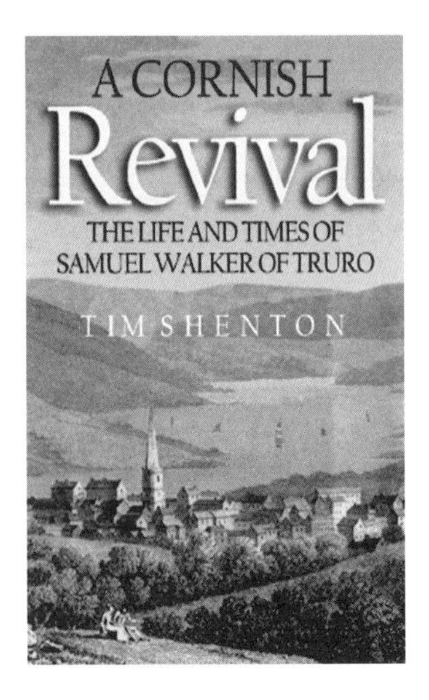

A Cornish Revival: The Life and Times of Samuel Walker of Truro

Author: Tim Shenton

Evangelical Press

ISBN-13: 978 0 8523 4522 1

'Tim Shenton has brought Samuel Walker to life in an authentic and graphic way ... He puts each aspect of Walker's life into context and does not fail to convey the challenge of his life and ministry. I thoroughly recommend this biography. It is suitable and edifying for ministers and all who would seek to live as God would have us live.'

English Churchman

'Tim Shenton's biography of a gallant, practical church leader reminds us of the potential for renewal in our own, sometimes discouraging, times. Well researched, it is inspirational and very useful.'

Christian Herald

'A first-rate insight into the times.'

Metropolitan Tabernacle

'This excellent biography contains many extracts from Walker's sermons and published writings, and also from his correspondence with other ministers and acquaintances. There are also samples of his counsel and extracts from his personal diaries, many of which are instructive, searching and edifying ... Tim Shenton has put us all in his debt by writing this informative and edifying book that cannot fail to bless and encourage the thoughtful reader.'

Evangelicals Now

'Mr Shenton paints an attractive, challenging and encouraging portrait.'

The Banner of Truth

Christmas Evans: The Life and Times of the One-Eyed Preacher of Wales

Author: Tim Shenton

Evangelical Press

ISBN-13: 978 0 8523 4483 5

'This book truly warms the heart and is a timely reminder of what the Lord can do through the simple preaching of the gospel.'

Evangelical Presbyterian Magazine

'Tim Shenton has done Baptists and the Church of Jesus Christ a great favour in producing this new and definitive biography.'

The Baptist Page

'A well researched and excellent biography ... a spiritually uplifting work.'

Peace and Truth

'Tim Shenton's extensive, thorough and well-documented research has produced the most accurate work on Christmas Evans that has ever appeared; it is certainly going to be the standard work for many years to come. It is written in a style everyone can enjoy, and with a spiritual insight that makes every page worthwhile.'

Stuart Olyott